Y0-DJQ-713

"The LORD bless you
and keep you;
the LORD make his face shine upon you
and be gracious to you;
the LORD turn his face toward you
and give you peace."

NUMBERS 6:24–26

Promises for Students from the New International Version
ISBN-10: 0-310-81138-4
ISBN-13: 978-0-310-81138-1

Requests for information should be addressed to:
Inspirio, The gift group of Zondervan
Grand Rapids, Michigan 49530
www.inspiriogifts.com

Developed and produced by The Livingstone Corporation
Update by Snapdragon Editorial Group, Inc.

Project staff: Paige Haley, Christopher D. Hudson
Project Manager: Tom Dean
Design Manager: Michael J. Williams
Production Management: Bev Stout
Designer: Kirk DouPonce, DogEared Design

Printed in China
06 07 08 / 4 3 2 1

PROMISES

FOR STUDENTS

FROM THE NIV

inspirio™

Dear Student,

As you set out on the new path before you,

cling to the promises of God. He will be faithful

to you and will enrich your life with his good

and perfect gifts. Because of God, you have

great cause for confidence.

"I know the plans I have for you," declares the LORD, "plans to prosper you and not to harm you, plans to give you hope and a future. Then you will call upon me and come and pray to me, and I will listen to you. You will seek me and find me when you seek me with all your heart."

JEREMIAH 29:11–13

TABLE OF CONTENTS

6. HOW DO YOU GROW IN FAITH?
Promises about the Christian Life

7. WHAT DOES GOD GIVE TO HIS CHILDREN?
Promises about God's Perfect Gifts for You

8. HOW DOES GOD VALUE YOUR RELATIONSHIPS?
Promises for Your Friends and Family

9. HOW SHOULD YOU LIVE NOW?
Promises for the Christian Walk

Thank you, God,

for the rich promises from your Word.

Your Word is true and offers light

for my path. Thank you that I can depend

on you at all times and for every need,

because I can trust in who you are.

You never change.

CAN YOU DEPEND ON GOD?

Promises about Who God Is

GOD IS LOVING

NEHEMIAH 9:17
You are a forgiving God, gracious and compassionate,
slow to anger and abounding in love.

JEREMIAH 31:3
The LORD appeared to us in the past, saying:
"I have loved you with an everlasting love;
I have drawn you with loving-kindness."

PSALM 145:8
The LORD is gracious and compassionate,
slow to anger and rich in love.

LAMENTATIONS 3:22–23
Because of the LORD's great love we are not consumed,
for his compassions never fail.
They are new every morning;
great is your faithfulness.

ISAIAH 40:11

The LORD tends his flock like a shepherd:
    He gathers the lambs in his arms
and carries them close to his heart;
    he gently leads those that have young.

EPHESIANS 2:4–5

Because of his great love for us, God, who is rich in mercy,
made us alive with Christ even when we were dead in
transgressions—it is by grace you have been saved.

ISAIAH 54:10

"Though the mountains be shaken
    and the hills be removed,
yet my unfailing love for you will not be shaken
    nor my covenant of peace be removed,"
    says the LORD, who has compassion on you.

1 CHRONICLES 16:34

Give thanks to the LORD, for he is good;
    his love endures forever.

PSALM 33:18
The eyes of the LORD are on those who fear him,
     on those whose hope is in his unfailing love.

PSALM 36:5, 7
Your love, O LORD, reaches to the heavens,
     your faithfulness to the skies....
     How priceless is your unfailing love!
Both high and low among men
     find refuge in the shadow of your wings.

PSALM 63:3–4
Because your love is better than life, O LORD,
     my lips will glorify you.
I will praise you as long as I live,
     And in your name I will lift up may hands.

PSALM 103:11
As high as the heavens are above the earth,
     so great is God's love for those who fear him.

GOD IS LOVING

EPHESIANS 3:17–19

I pray that you, being rooted and established in love, may have power, together with all the saints, to grasp how wide and long and high and deep is the love of Christ, and to know this love that surpasses knowledge—that you may be filled to the measure of all the fullness of God.

1 JOHN 3:16

This is how we know what love is: Jesus Christ laid down his life for us.

1 JOHN 4:16

We know and rely on the love God has for us. God is love. Whoever lives in love lives in God, and God in him.

JOHN 3:16

God so loved the world that he gave his one and only Son, that whoever believes in him shall not perish but have eternal life.

ROMANS 5:8

God demonstrates his own love for us in this: While we were still sinners, Christ died for us.

2 JOHN 1:3

Grace, mercy and peace from God the Father and from Jesus Christ, the Father's Son, will be with us in truth and love.

TITUS 3:4–5

When the kindness and love of God our Savior appeared, he saved us, not because of righteous things we had done, but because of his mercy.

ROMANS 8:38–39

I am convinced that neither death nor life, neither angels nor demons, neither the present nor the future, nor any powers, neither height nor depth, nor anything else in all creation, will be able to separate us from the love of God that is in Christ Jesus our LORD.

ZEPHANIAH 3:17

The LORD your God is with you,
    he is mighty to save.
He will take great delight in you,
    he will quiet you with his love,
    he will rejoice over you with singing.

GOD IS LOVING

ROMANS 5:5
God has poured out his love into our hearts by the Holy Spirit, whom he has given us.

1 JOHN 4:10–12
This is love: not that we loved God, but that he loved us and sent his Son as an atoning sacrifice for our sins. Dear friends, since God so loved us, we also ought to love one another. No one has ever seen God; but if we love one another, God lives in us and his love is made complete in us.

2 THESSALONIANS 2:16–17
May our LORD Jesus Christ himself and God our Father, who loved us and by his grace gave us eternal encouragement and good hope, encourage your hearts and strengthen you in every good deed and word.

EPHESIANS 5:2
Live a life of love, just as Christ loved us and gave himself up for us as a fragrant offering and sacrifice to God.

1 JOHN 4:18
There is no fear in love. But perfect love drives out fear.

1 JOHN 3:1
How great is the love the Father has lavished on us,
that we should be called children of God! And that is
what we are!

EPHESIANS 1:4–6
In love God predestined us to be adopted as his sons
through Jesus Christ, in accordance with his pleasure
and will—to the praise of his glorious grace, which he
has freely given us in the One he loves.

2 CORINTHIANS 13:14
May the grace of the LORD Jesus Christ, and the love of
God, and the fellowship of the Holy Spirit be with you.

PSALM 103:17
From everlasting to everlasting
    the LORD's love is with those who fear him,
    and his righteousness with their children's children.

GOD IS LOVING

1 JOHN 4:9

This is how God showed his love among us: He sent his one and only Son into the world that we might live through him.

PSALM 136:26

Give thanks to the God of heaven.
    His love endures forever.

PSALM 147:11

The LORD delights in those who fear him,
    who put their hope in his unfailing love.

PSALM 25:6–7

Remember, O LORD, your great mercy and love,
    for they are from of old.
Remember not the sins of my youth
    and my rebellious ways;
according to your love remember me,
    for you are good, O LORD.

GOD IS GRACIOUS

PSALM 86:15
You, O LORD, are a compassionate and gracious God,
    slow to anger, abounding in love and faithfulness.

JAMES 5:11
The LORD is full of compassion and mercy.

ISAIAH 30:18
The LORD longs to be gracious to you;
    he rises to show you compassion.
For the LORD is a God of justice.
    Blessed are all who wait for him!

ISAIAH 33:2
O LORD, be gracious to us;
    we long for you.
Be our strength every morning,
    our salvation in time of distress.

ISAIAH 38:17
In your love you kept me
    from the pit of destruction, O LORD;
you have put all my sins
    behind your back.

TITUS 3:5-6
God saved us, not because of righteous things we had
done, but because of his mercy. He saved us through
the washing of rebirth and renewal by the Holy Spirit,
whom he poured out on us generously through Jesus
Christ our Savior.

1 PETER 1:3
Praise be to the God and Father of our LORD Jesus
Christ! In his great mercy he has given us new birth
into a living hope through the resurrection of Jesus
Christ from the dead.

PSALM 116:1
I love the LORD, for he heard my voice;
    he heard my cry for mercy.

PSALM 51:1
Have mercy on me, O God,
    according to your unfailing love;
according to your great compassion
    blot out my transgressions.

MICAH 7:18
Who is a God like you,
who pardons sin and forgives the transgression
of the remnant of his inheritance?
You do not stay angry forever
    but delight to show mercy.

2 CORINTHIANS 12:9
The LORD said to me, "My grace is sufficient for you,
for my power is made perfect in weakness." Therefore
I will boast all the more gladly about my weaknesses,
so that Christ's power may rest on me.

2 PETER 3:18
Grow in the grace and knowledge of our LORD and
Savior Jesus Christ. To him be glory both now and
forever! Amen.

GOD IS GRACIOUS

2 CHRONICLES 30:9
The LORD your God is gracious and compassionate. He will not turn his face from you if you return to him.

EPHESIANS 1:3–8
Praise be to the God and Father of our LORD Jesus Christ, who has blessed us in the heavenly realms with every spiritual blessing in Christ. For he chose us in him before the creation of the world to be holy and blameless in his sight. In love he predestined us to be adopted as his sons through Jesus Christ, in accordance with his pleasure and will—to the praise of his glorious grace, which he has freely given us in the One he loves. In Christ we have redemption through his blood, the forgiveness of sins, in accordance with the riches of God's grace that he lavished on us with all wisdom and understanding.

1 CORINTHIANS 15:10
By the grace of God I am what I am, and his grace to me was not without effect.

GOD IS STRONG

PSALM 46:1–3
God is our refuge and strength,
    an ever-present help in trouble.
Therefore we will not fear, though the earth give way
    and the mountains fall into the heart of the sea,
though its waters roar and foam
    and the mountains quake with their surging.

PSALM 73:26
My flesh and my heart may fail,
    but God is the strength of my heart
    and my portion forever.

PROVERBS 18:10
The name of the LORD is a strong tower;
    the righteous run to it and are safe.

PSALM 18:1
I love you, O LORD, my strength.

PSALM 84:5
Blessed are those whose strength is in you, O LORD.

HABAKKUK 3:19
The Sovereign LORD is my strength;
    he makes my feet like the feet of a deer,
    he enables me to go on the heights.

EPHESIANS 6:10–13
Be strong in the LORD and in his mighty power. Put on the full armor of God so that you can take your stand against the devil's schemes. For our struggle is not against flesh and blood, but against the rulers, against the authorities, against the powers of this dark world and against the spiritual forces of evil in the heavenly realms. Therefore put on the full armor of God, so that when the day of evil comes, you may be able to stand your ground, and after you have done everything, to stand.

PSALM 59:9
O my Strength, I watch for you;
    you, O God, are my fortress, my loving God.

PSALM 27:1
The LORD is my light and my salvation—
    whom shall I fear?
The LORD is the stronghold of my life—
    of whom shall I be afraid?

2 SAMUEL 22:33
It is God who arms me with
    strength and makes my way perfect.

PSALM 16:5,8
LORD, you have assigned me my portion and my cup;
    you have made my lot secure....
I have set the LORD always before me.
    Because he is at my right hand,
        I will not be shaken.

PSALM 55:22
Cast your cares on the LORD
    and he will sustain you;
        he will never let the righteous fall.

GOD IS STRONG

PSALM 59:16

I will sing of your strength, O LORD,
in the morning I will sing of your love;
for you are my fortress,
my refuge in times of trouble.

HEBREWS 13:6

We say with confidence,
"The LORD is my helper; I will not be afraid.
What can man do to me?"

DEUTERONOMY 33:27

The eternal God is your refuge,
and underneath are the everlasting arms.

2 SAMUEL 22:31

As for God, his way is perfect;
the word of the LORD is flawless.
He is a shield
for all who take refuge in him.

PSALM 4:8

I will lie down and sleep in peace,
for you alone, O LORD,
make me dwell in safety.

PSALM 17:7–8

Show the wonder of your great love, O LORD,
you who save by your right hand
those who take refuge in you from their foes.
Keep me as the apple of your eye;
hide me in the shadow of your wings.

PSALM 32:7

You are my hiding place, O God;
you will protect me from trouble
and surround me with songs of deliverance.

PSALM 116:6

The LORD protects the simplehearted;
when I was in great need, he saved me.

GOD IS STRONG

PSALM 46:5-7
God is within [Jerusalem], she will not fall;
    God will help her at break of day.
Nations are in uproar, kingdoms fall;
    he lifts his voice, the earth melts.

The LORD Almighty is with us;
    the God of Jacob is our fortress.

PSALM 91:14-15
"Because he loves me," says the LORD, "I will rescue him;
    I will protect him, for he acknowledges my name.
He will call upon me, and I will answer him;
    I will be with him in trouble,
    I will deliver him and honor him."

ISAIAH 41:10
"Do not fear, for I am with you;
    do not be dismayed, for I am your God.
I will strengthen you and help you;
    I will uphold you with my righteous right hand."

2 THESSALONIANS 3:3
The LORD is faithful, and he will strengthen and protect
you from the evil one.

ISAIAH 43:1–2
"Fear not, for I have redeemed you;
    I have summoned you by name; you are mine.
When you pass through the waters,
    I will be with you;
and when you pass through the rivers,
    they will not sweep over you.
When you walk through the fire,
    you will not be burned;
    the flames will not set you ablaze," says the LORD.

GOD IS STRONG

NAHUM 1:7
The LORD is good,
a refuge in times of trouble.
He cares for those who trust in him.

NEHEMIAH 8:10
"The joy of the LORD is your strength."

PHILIPPIANS 4:13
I can do everything through God who gives me strength.

PSALM 28:7
The LORD is my strength and my shield;
my heart trusts in him, and I am helped.

ISAIAH 33:2
O LORD, be gracious to us;
we long for you.
Be our strength every morning,
our salvation in time of distress.

GOD IS FAITHFUL

PSALM 100:5
The LORD is good and his love endures forever;
   his faithfulness continues through all generations.

DEUTERONOMY 7:9
Know therefore that the LORD your God is God; he is
the faithful God, keeping his covenant of love to a
thousand generations of those who love him and keep
his commands.

PSALM 91:1–2, 4
He who dwells in the shelter of the Most High
   will rest in the shadow of the Almighty.
I will say of the LORD, "He is my refuge and my fortress,
   my God, in whom I trust." ...
He will cover you with his feathers,
   and under his wings you will find refuge;
   his faithfulness will be your shield and rampart.

1 JOHN 1:9

If we confess our sins, God is faithful and just and will
forgive us our sins and purify us from all unrighteousness.

PSALM 108:4

Great is your love, O LORD, higher than the heavens;
    your faithfulness reaches to the skies.

PSALM 121:3–8

The LORD will not let your foot slip—
    he who watches over you will not slumber;
indeed, he who watches over Israel
    will neither slumber nor sleep.

The LORD watches over you—
    the LORD is your shade at your right hand;
the sun will not harm you by day,
    nor the moon by night.

The LORD will keep you from all harm—
    he will watch over your life;
the LORD will watch over your coming and going
    both now and forevermore.

LAMENTATIONS 3:22-23
Because of the LORD's great love we are not con-
sumed,
    for his compassions never fail.
They are new every morning;
    great is your faithfulness.

1 CORINTHIANS 1:9
God, who has called you into fellowship with his Son
Jesus Christ our LORD, is faithful.

2 THESSALONIANS 3:3
The LORD is faithful, and he will strengthen and protect you from the evil one.

DEUTERONOMY 32:4
God is the Rock, his works are perfect,
    and all his ways are just.
A faithful God who does no wrong,
    upright and just is he.

GOD IS FAITHFUL

PSALM 33:4
The word of the LORD is right and true;
　　he is faithful in all he does.

PSALM 86:15
You, O LORD, are a compassionate and gracious God,
　　slow to anger, abounding in love and faithfulness.

PSALM 115:1
Not to us, O LORD, not to us
　　but to your name be the glory,
　　because of your love and faithfulness.

PSALM 138:8
The LORD will fulfill his purpose for me;
　　your love, O LORD, endures forever—
　　do not abandon the works of your hands.

1 CORINTHIANS 10:13

God is faithful; he will not let you be tempted beyond what you can bear. But when you are tempted, he will also provide a way out so that you can stand up under it.

1 THESSALONIANS 5:23–24

May God himself, the God of peace, sanctify you through and through. May your whole spirit, soul and body be kept blameless at the coming of our LORD Jesus Christ. The one who calls you is faithful and he will do it.

2 TIMOTHY 2:13

If we are faithless,
    Christ will remain faithful.

HEBREWS 10:23

Let us hold unswervingly to the hope we profess, for God who promised is faithful.

ACTS 14:17

God has not left himself without testimony: He has shown kindness by giving you rain from heaven and crops in their seasons; he provides you with plenty of food and fills your hearts with joy.

GOD IS FAITHFUL

PSALM 23:1

The LORD is my shepherd, I shall not be in want.

2 CORINTHIANS 9:8

God is able to make all grace abound to you, so that in all things at all times, having all that you need, you will abound in every good work.

PHILIPPIANS 4:19

God will meet all your needs according to his glorious riches in Christ Jesus.

PSALM 111:7–8

The works of [God's] hands are faithful and just;
    all his precepts are trustworthy.
They are steadfast for ever and ever.
    done in faithfulness and uprightness.

GOD IS COMPASSIONATE

PSALM 145:8
The LORD is gracious and compassionate,
    slow to anger and rich in love.

ISAIAH 30:18
The LORD longs to be gracious to you;
    he rises to show you compassion.
For the LORD is a God of justice.
    Blessed are all who wait for him!

PSALM 119:156
Your compassion is great, O LORD;
    preserve my life according to your laws.

ISAIAH 54:10
"Though the mountains be shaken
    and the hills be removed,
yet my unfailing love for you will not be shaken
    nor my covenant of peace be removed,"
    says the LORD, who has compassion on you.

PSALM 145:9
The Lord is good to all;
    he has compassion on all he has made.

HOSEA 2:19
"I will betroth you to me forever;
    I will betroth you in righteousness and justice,
    in love and compassion,"
        declares the Lord.

EXODUS 33:19
The Lord said, "I will cause all my goodness to pass in front of you, and I will proclaim my name, the Lord, in your presence. I will have mercy on whom I will have mercy, and I will have compassion on whom I will have compassion."

PSALM 111:4
God has caused his wonders to be remembered;
    the Lord is gracious and compassionate.

PSALM 103:2–5
Praise the LORD, O my soul,
    and forget not all his benefits—
who forgives all your sins
    and heals all your diseases,
who redeems your life from the pit
    and crowns you with love and compassion,
who satisfies your desires with good things
    so that your youth is renewed like the eagle's.

2 CORINTHIANS 1:3
Praise be to the God and Father of our LORD Jesus Christ,
the Father of compassion and the God of all comfort.

EPHESIANS 4:32
Be kind and compassionate to one another, forgiving
each other, just as in Christ God forgave you.

JAMES 5:11
The LORD is full of compassion and mercy.

GOD IS COMPASSIONATE

ISAIAH 49:10, 13

They will neither hunger nor thirst,
nor will the desert heat or the sun beat upon
them.
God who has compassion on them will guide them
and lead them beside springs of water....
Shout for joy, O heavens;
rejoice, O earth;
burst into song, O mountains!
For the LORD comforts his people
and will have compassion on his afflicted ones.

LAMENTATIONS 3:32

God will show compassion,
so great is his unfailing love.

ISAIAH 54:8

"With everlasting kindness
I will have compassion on you,"
says the LORD your Redeemer.

PSALM 103:11–13

As high as the heavens are above the earth,
	so great is God's love for those who fear him;
as far as the east is from the west,
	so far has he removed our transgressions from us.
As a father has compassion on his children,
	so the LORD has compassion on those who fear him.

MICAH 7:18–19

Who is a God like you,
	who pardons sin and forgives the transgression
	of the remnant of his inheritance?
You do not stay angry forever
	but delight to show mercy.
You will again have compassion on us;
	you will tread our sins underfoot
	and hurl all our iniquities into the depths of the sea.

GOD IS COMPASSIONATE

HOSEA 11:4

"I led them with cords of human kindness,
    with ties of love;
I lifted the yoke from their neck
    and bent down to feed them,"
        declares the LORD.

PSALM 18:6, 16–17

In my distress I called to the LORD;
    I cried to my God for help.
From his temple he heard my voice;
    my cry came before him, into his ears.
He reached down from on high and took hold of me;
    he drew me out of deep waters.
He rescued me from my powerful enemy.

WHO IS GOD TO YOU?

Promises about God's Role in Your Life

*Thank you, my L*ORD*, that you are a personal*
God. You made me in your own image and
designed me to have a relationship with you.
Thank you that you are all things to me and
you meet my every need. Every time I seek you,
you reveal yourself to me in new and
refreshing ways.

GOD IS YOUR SAVIOR

JOHN 3:16
God so loved the world that he gave his one and only
Son, that whoever believes in him shall not perish but
have eternal life.

ROMANS 5:8
God demonstrates his own love for us in this: While
we were still sinners, Christ died for us.

1 JOHN 4:10
This is love: not that we loved God, but that he loved
us and sent his Son as an atoning sacrifice for our sins.

ISAIAH 53:5
He was pierced for our transgressions,
    he was crushed for our iniquities;
the punishment that brought us peace was upon him,
    and by his wounds we are healed.

1 JOHN 2:2

Jesus Christ is the atoning sacrifice for our sins, and not only for ours but also for the sins of the whole world.

1 PETER 1:18–19

You know that it was not with perishable things such as silver or gold that you were redeemed ... but with the precious blood of Christ, a lamb without blemish or defect.

ISAIAH 1:18

"Come now, let us reason together,"
     says the LORD.
"Though your sins are like scarlet,
     they shall be as white as snow;
though they are red as crimson,
     they shall be like wool."

ACTS 2:38

Peter said, "Repent and be baptized, every one of you, in the name of Jesus Christ for the forgiveness of your sins. And you will receive the gift of the Holy Spirit."

Isaiah 43:25

"I, even I, am he who blots out
    your transgressions, for my own sake,
    and remembers your sins no more,"
        declares the LORD.

Ephesians 1:7

In Christ we have redemption through his blood, the
forgiveness of sins, in accordance with the riches of
God's grace.

Colossians 2:13–14

When you were dead in your sins and in the uncircumcision of your sinful nature, God made you alive
with Christ. He forgave us all our sins, having canceled the written code, with its regulations, that was
against us and that stood opposed to us; he took it
away, nailing it to the cross.

1 John 1:9

If we confess our sins, God is faithful and just and will
forgive us our sins and purify us from all unrighteousness.

GOD IS YOUR SAVIOR

EZEKIEL 36:26
God said, "I will give you a new heart and put a new spirit in you; I will remove from you your heart of stone and give you a heart of flesh."

LAMENTATIONS 3:57–58
You came near when I called you,
    and you said, "Do not fear."

O LORD, you took up my case;
    you redeemed my life.

ACTS 10:43
All the prophets testify about Jesus that everyone who believes in him receives forgiveness of sins through his name.

2 CORINTHIANS 5:17
If anyone is in Christ, he is a new creation; the old has gone, the new has come!

EPHESIANS 2:4-5

Because of his great love for us, God, who is rich in mercy, made us alive with Christ even when we were dead in transgressions—it is by grace you have been saved.

PSALM 62:1-2

My soul finds rest in God alone;
    my salvation comes from him.
He alone is my rock and my salvation;
    he is my fortress, I will never be shaken.

ISAIAH 44:22

"I have swept away your offenses like a cloud,
    your sins like the morning mist.
Return to me,
    for I have redeemed you," declares the LORD.

JOHN 3:36

Whoever believes in the Son has eternal life.

GOD IS YOUR SAVIOR

2 CORINTHIANS 6:2
God says,
"In the time of my favor I heard you,
    and in the day of salvation I helped you."
I tell you, now is the time of God's favor, now is the
day of salvation.

EPHESIANS 2:13
Now in Christ Jesus you who once were far away have
been brought near through the blood of Christ.

COLOSSIANS 1:13–14
God has rescued us from the dominion of darkness
and brought us into the kingdom of the Son he loves,
in whom we have redemption, the forgiveness of sins.

TITUS 3:5
God saved us, not because of righteous things we had
done, but because of his mercy. He saved us through
the washing of rebirth and renewal by the Holy Spirit.

1 PETER 2:24
Christ himself bore our sins in his body on the tree, so
that we might die to sins and live for righteousness;
by his wounds you have been healed.

JOHN 14:6

Jesus said, "I am the way and the truth and the life. No one comes to the Father except through me."

1 JOHN 5:18

We know that anyone born of God does not continue to sin; the one who was born of God keeps him safe, and the evil one cannot harm him.

1 PETER 1:3-5

Praise be to the God and Father of our LORD Jesus Christ! In his great mercy he has given us new birth into a living hope through the resurrection of Jesus Christ from the dead, and into an inheritance that can never perish, spoil or fade—kept in heaven for you, who through faith are shielded by God's power until the coming of the salvation that is ready to be revealed in the last time.

JOHN 4:13-14

Jesus answered, "Everyone who drinks this water will be thirsty again, but whoever drinks the water I give him will never thirst. Indeed, the water I give him will become in him a spring of water welling up to eternal life."

GOD IS YOUR SAVIOR

ROMANS 5:17

If, by the trespass of the one man, death reigned through that one man, how much more will those who receive God's abundant provision of grace and of the gift of righteousness reign in life through the one man, Jesus Christ.

PSALM 40:2

He lifted me out of the slimy pit,
    out of the mud and mire;
he set my feet on a rock
    and gave me a firm place to stand.

1 TIMOTHY 2:3–6

God our Savior ... wants all me to be saved and to come to a knowledge of the truth. For there is one God and one mediator between God and men, the man Christ Jesus, who gave himself as a ransom for all men.

GOD IS YOUR SHEPHERD

PSALM 23:1
The LORD is my shepherd, I shall not be in want.

JOHN 10:14-16
Jesus said, "I am the good shepherd; I know my sheep and my sheep know me—just as the Father knows me and I know the Father—and I lay down my life for the sheep. I have other sheep that are not of this sheep pen. I must bring them also. They too will listen to my voice, and there shall be one flock and one shepherd."

PSALM 28:9
Save your people and bless your inheritance,
        O LORD;
    be their shepherd and carry them forever.

PSALM 78:52
God brought his people out like a flock;
    he led them like sheep through the desert.

PSALM 100:3
Know that the LORD is God.
    It is he who made us, and we are his.

PSALM 95:7
He is our God
>and we are the people of his pasture,
>the flock under his care.

ISAIAH 40:11
The LORD tends his flock like a shepherd:
>He gathers the lambs in his arms
and carries them close to his heart;
>he gently leads those that have young.

JEREMIAH 23:3
"I myself will gather the remnant of my flock out of all the countries where I have driven them and will bring them back to their pasture, where they will be fruitful and increase in number," declares the LORD.

EZEKIEL 34:15-16
"I myself will tend my sheep and have them lie down," declares the Sovereign LORD. "I will search for the lost and bring back the strays. I will bind up the injured and strengthen the weak."

JEREMIAH 31:10
Hear the word of the Lord, O nations;
      proclaim it in distant coastlands:
"He who scattered Israel will gather them
      and will watch over his flock like a shepherd."

EZEKIEL 34:11–12
This is what the Sovereign Lord says: "I myself will
search for my sheep and look after them. As a shepherd looks after his scattered flock when he is with
them, so will I look after my sheep. I will rescue them
from all the places where they were scattered on a day
of clouds and darkness."

EZEKIEL 34:31
"You my sheep, the sheep of my pasture, are people,
and I am your God," declares the Sovereign Lord.

MARK 6:34
When Jesus ... saw a large crowd, he had compassion
on them, because they were like sheep without a
shepherd. So he began teaching them many things.

GOD IS YOUR SHEPHERD

ZECHARIAH 9:16
The LORD their God will save them on that day
as the flock of his people.
They will sparkle in his land
like jewels in a crown.

LUKE 12:32
Jesus said to his disciples, "Do not be afraid, little
flock, for your Father has been pleased to give you
the kingdom."

HEBREWS 13:20–21
May the God of peace, who through the blood of the
eternal covenant brought back from the dead our
LORD Jesus, that great Shepherd of the sheep, equip
you with everything good for doing his will, and may
he work in us what is pleasing to him, through Jesus
Christ, to whom be glory for ever and ever.

1 PETER 2:25
You were like sheep going astray, but now you have
returned to the Shepherd and Overseer of your souls.

Revelation 7:17

The Lamb at the center of the throne will be their shepherd;

he will lead them to springs of living water. And God will wipe away every tear from their eyes.

John 10:27–30

Jesus said, "My sheep listen to my voice; I know them, and they follow me. I give them eternal life, and they shall never perish; no one can snatch them out of my hand. My Father, who has given them to me, is greater than all; no one can snatch them out of my Father's hand. I and the Father are one."

John 10:11

Jesus said, "I am the good shepherd. The good shepherd lays down his life for the sheep."

Matthew 6:26

Jesus said to his disciples, "Look at the birds of the air; they do not sow or reap or store away in barns, and yet your heavenly Father feeds them. Are you not much more valuable than they?"

GOD IS YOUR SHEPHERD

PSALM 91:1–2, 4
He who dwells in the shelter of the Most High
    will rest in the shadow of the Almighty.
I will say of the LORD, "He is my refuge and my fortress,
    my God, in whom I trust." …
He will cover you with his feathers,
    and under his wings you will find refuge;
    his faithfulness will be your shield and rampart.

PSALM 121:5–8
The LORD watches over you—
    the LORD is your shade at your right hand;
the sun will not harm you by day,
    nor the moon by night.

The LORD will keep you from all harm—
    he will watch over your life;
the LORD will watch over your coming and going
    both now and forevermore.

GOD IS YOUR FRIEND

JOHN 15:15
Jesus said, "I no longer call you servants, because a servant does not know his master's business. Instead, I have called you friends, for everything that I learned from my Father I have made known to you."

HOSEA 11:4
"I led them with cords of human kindness,
    with ties of love;
I lifted the yoke from their neck
    and bent down to feed them,"
        declares the LORD.

JOHN 14:23
Jesus said, "If anyone loves me, he will obey my teaching. My Father will love him, and we will come to him and make our home with him."

JEREMIAH 15:15
You understand, O LORD;
    remember me and care for me.

JAMES 2:23
The scripture was fulfilled that says, "Abraham believed God, and it was credited to him as righteousness," and he was called God's friend.

REVELATION 3:20
Jesus said, "Here I am! I stand at the door and knock. If anyone hears my voice and opens the door, I will come in and eat with him, and he with me."

1 CORINTHIANS 1:9
God, who has called you into fellowship with his Son Jesus Christ our LORD, is faithful.

1 PETER 5:7
Cast all your anxiety on God because he cares for you.

1 JOHN 1:3
Our fellowship is with the Father and with his Son, Jesus Christ.

DEUTERONOMY 30:20
Love the LORD your God, listen to his voice, and hold fast to him. For the LORD is your life.

JOHN 14:21

Jesus said, "He who loves me will be loved by my
Father, and I too will love him and show myself to him."

PSALM 27:10

Though my father and mother forsake me,
    the LORD will receive me.

JOHN 14:18

Jesus said, "I will not leave you as orphans; I will
come to you."

JOHN 15:12-14

Jesus said, "Love each other as I have loved you.
Greater love has no one than this, that he lay down
his life for his friends. You are my friends if you do
what I command."

PROVERBS 18:24

There is a friend who sticks closer than a brother.

ISAIAH 43:4

"You are precious and honored in my sight, and ... I
love you," says the LORD.

GOD IS YOUR FRIEND

MATTHEW 28:20
Jesus said to his disciples, "And surely I am with you always, to the very end of the age."

GENESIS 28:15
"I am with you and will watch over you wherever you go, and I will bring you back to this land. I will not leave you until I have done what I have promised you," the LORD told Jacob.

JOHN 15:16
Jesus said, "You did not choose me, but I chose you and appointed you to go and bear fruit--fruit that will last. Then the Father will give you whatever you ask in my name."

GOD IS YOUR LORD

PHILIPPIANS 2:9–11
God exalted Christ to the highest place
    and gave him the name that is above every name,
that at the name of Jesus every knee should bow,
    in heaven and on earth and under the earth,
and every tongue confess that Jesus Christ is LORD,
    to the glory of God the Father.

ROMANS 10:9
If you confess with your mouth, "Jesus is LORD," and
believe in your heart that God raised him from the
dead, you will be saved.

ISAIAH 50:7
Because the Sovereign LORD helps me,
    I will not be disgraced.
Therefore have I set my face like flint,
    and I know I will not be put to shame.

ACTS 2:25
David said about God:
"I saw the LORD always before me.
    Because he is at my right hand,
    I will not be shaken."

ACTS 2:36
Let all Israel be assured of this: God has made this
Jesus... both LORD and Christ.

ROMANS 14:8
If we live, we live to the LORD; and if we die, we die
to the LORD. So, whether we live or die, we belong to
the LORD.

PSALM 16:2
I said to the LORD, "You are my Lord;
    apart from you I have no good thing."

PSALM 89:8
O LORD God Almighty, who is like you?
    You are mighty, O LORD, and your faithfulness
    surrounds you.

JEREMIAH 15:16
When your words came, I ate them;
they were my joy and my heart's delight,
for I bear your name,
O LORD God Almighty.

HOSEA 12:5
The LORD God Almighty,
the LORD is his name of renown!

ACTS 17:27
God is not far from each one of us.

AMOS 4:13
He who forms the mountains,
creates the wind,
and reveals his thoughts to man,
he who turns dawn to darkness,
and treads the high places of the earth—
the LORD God Almighty is his name.

GOD IS YOUR LORD

REVELATION 4:8
> Holy, holy, holy
> is the LORD God Almighty,
> who was, and is, and is to come.

REVELATION 11:17
> "We give thanks to you, LORD God Almighty,
>   the One who is and who was,
> because you have taken your great power
>   and have begun to reign."

REVELATION 15:3
> "Great and marvelous are your deeds,
>   LORD God Almighty.
> Just and true are your ways,
>   King of the ages."

ROMANS 6:22
Now that you have been set free from sin and have become slaves to God, the benefit you reap leads to holiness, and the result is eternal life.

PSALM 84:11
The LORD God is a sun and shield;
    the LORD bestows favor and honor;
no good thing does he withhold
    from those whose walk is blameless.

PSALM 11:7
The LORD is righteous,
    he loves justice;
    upright men will see his face.

PSALM 103:6
The LORD works righteousness
    and justice for all the oppressed.

PSALM 139:9–10
If I rise on the wings of the dawn,
    if I settle on the far side of the sea,
even there your hand will guide me, O LORD,
    your right hand will hold me fast.

GOD IS YOUR LORD

ISAIAH 43:2–3
This is what the LORD says,
"When you pass through the waters,
    I will be with you;
and when you pass through the rivers,
    they will not sweep over you.
When you walk through the fire,
    you will not be burned;
    the flames will not set you ablaze.
For I am the LORD, your God,
    the Holy One of Israel, your Savior."

PSALM 145:18
The LORD is near to all who call on him,
    to all who call on him in truth.

DEUTERONOMY 31:6
"Be strong and courageous. Do not be afraid or terrified ... for the LORD your God goes with you; he will
never leave you nor forsake you."

DEUTERONOMY 4:7
What other nation is so great as to have their gods near them the way the LORD our God is near us whenever we pray to him?

PSALM 119:137
Righteous are you, O LORD,
    and your laws are right.

REVELATION 11:15
The kingdom of the world has become the kingdom
    of our LORD and of his Christ,
    and he will reign for ever and ever.

ROMANS 4:20–25
Abraham did not waver through unbelief regarding the promise of God, but was strengthened in his faith and gave glory to God, being fully persuaded that God had power to do what he had promised. This is why "it was credited to him as righteousness." The words "it was credited to him" were written not for him alone, but also for us, to whom God will credit righteousness—for us who believe in him who raised Jesus our LORD from the dead. He was delivered over to death for our sins and was raised to life for our justification.

GOD IS YOUR LORD

PSALM 145:17

The LORD is righteous in all his ways
and loving toward all he has made.

1 CHRONICLES 16:25–27

Great is the LORD and most worthy of praise;
he is to be feared above all gods.
For all the gods of the nations are idols,
but the LORD made the heavens.
Splendor and majesty are before him;
strength and joy in his dwelling place.

PSALM 99:2

Great is the LORD in Zion;
he is exalted over all the nations.
Let them praise your great and awesome name—
he is holy.

GOD IS YOUR FATHER

ISAIAH 64:8
O LORD, you are our Father.
We are the clay, you are the potter;
we are all the work of your hand.

2 CORINTHIANS 6:18
"I will be a Father to you,
and you will be my sons and daughters,"
says the Lord Almighty.

MATTHEW 5:16
Jesus said to his disciples, "Let your light shine before
men, that they may see your good deeds and praise
your Father in heaven."

MATTHEW 6:6
Jesus said to his disciples, "When you pray, go into
your room, close the door and pray to your Father,
who is unseen. Then your Father, who sees what is
done in secret, will reward you."

MATTHEW 6:14
Jesus said to his disciples, "If you forgive men when they sin against you, your heavenly Father will also forgive you."

JOHN 6:57
Jesus said, "Just as the living Father sent me and I live because of the Father, so the one who feeds on me will live because of me."

MATTHEW 6:26
Jesus said to his disciples, "Look at the birds of the air; they do not sow or reap or store away in barns, and yet your heavenly Father feeds them. Are you not much more valuable than they?"

LUKE 12:32
Jesus said to his disciples, "Do not be afraid, little flock, for your Father has been pleased to give you the kingdom."

MATTHEW 18:19
Jesus said, "If two of you on earth agree about anything you ask for, it will be done for you by my Father in heaven."

MATTHEW 7:11

Jesus said to his disciples, "If you ... know how to give good gifts to your children, how much more will your Father in heaven give good gifts to those who ask him!"

ISAIAH 9:6

To us a child is born,
>   to us a son is given,
>   and the government will be on his shoulders.
And he will be called
>   Wonderful Counselor, Mighty God,
>   Everlasting Father, Prince of Peace.

MATTHEW 10:29, 31

Jesus said, "Are not two sparrows sold for a penny? Yet not one of them will fall to the ground apart from the will of your Father.... So don't be afraid; you are worth more than many sparrows."

2 CORINTHIANS 1:3

Praise be to the God and Father of our LORD Jesus Christ, the Father of compassion and the God of all comfort.

GOD IS YOUR FATHER

1 CORINTHIANS 8:6

For us there is but one God, the Father, from whom all things came and for whom we live; and there is but one LORD, Jesus Christ, through whom all things came and through whom we live.

HEBREWS 12:9

We have all had human fathers who disciplined us and we respected them for it. How much more should we submit to the Father of our spirits and live!

JOHN 15:9

Jesus said, "As the Father has loved me, so have I loved you."

JOHN 14:6

Jesus said, "I am the way and the truth and the life. No one comes to the Father except through me."

JAMES 1:17

Every good and perfect gift is from above, coming down from the Father of the heavenly lights, who does not change like shifting shadows.

GALATIANS 3:26, 28
You are all sons of God through faith in Christ Jesus.
... There is neither Jew nor Greek, slave nor free, male
nor female, for you are all one in Christ Jesus.

1 JOHN 2:23
Whoever acknowledges the Son has the Father also.

EPHESIANS 5:1–2
Be imitators of God, therefore, as dearly loved children
and live a life of love, just as Christ loved us and gave
himself up for us as a fragrant offering and sacrifice
to God.

ROMANS 8:14–16
Those who are led by the Spirit of God are sons of God.
For you did not receive a spirit that makes you a slave
again to fear, but you received the Spirit of sonship. And
by him we cry, "*Abba*, Father." The Spirit himself testifies with our spirit that we are God's children.

1 JOHN 3:1
How great is the love the Father has lavished on us,
that we should be called children of God! And that is
what we are!

GOD IS YOUR FATHER

JOHN 1:12-13

To all who received Christ, to those who believed in his name, he gave the right to become children of God—children born not of natural descent, nor of human decision or a husband's will, but born of God.

1 JOHN 3:2

Dear friends, now we are children of God, and what we will be has not yet been made known. But we know that when he appears, we shall be like him, for we shall see him as he is.

PSALM 103:13

As a father has compassion on his children,
    so the LORD has compassion on those who fear him.

1 JOHN 5:2-4

This is how we know that we love the children of God: by loving God and carrying out his commands. This is love for God: to obey his commands. And his commands are not burdensome, for everyone born of God overcomes the world. This is the victory that has overcome the world, even our faith.

PSALM 2:7-9

I will proclaim the decree of the LORD:
>   He said to me, "You are my Son;
>   today I have become your Father.
Ask of me,
>   and I will make the nations your inheritance,
>   the ends of the earth your possession.
You will rule them with an iron scepter;
>   you will dash them to pieces like pottery."

PSALM 68:5

A father to the fatherless, a defender of widows,
>   is God in his holy dwelling.

PROVERBS 3:11-12

Do not despise the LORD's discipline
>   and do not resent his rebuke,
Because the LORD disciplines those he loves,
>   as a father the son he delights in.

GOD IS YOUR FATHER

1 JOHN 4:14–15
We have seen and testify that the Father has sent his
Son to be the Savior of the world. If anyone acknowledges that Jesus is the Son of God, God lives in him
and he in God.

GALATIANS 4:3–7
When we were children, we were in slavery under the
basic principles of the world. But when the time had
fully come, God sent his Son, born of a woman, born
under law, to redeem those under the law, that we
might receive the full rights of sons. Because you are
sons, God sent the Spirit of his Son into our hearts,
the Spirit who calls out, "*Abba*, Father." So you are no
longer a slave, but a son; and since you are a son,
God has made you also an heir.

DOES GOD HOLD YOUR FUTURE?

Promises about God's Guidance

Thank you, God, that you have engraved me on the palm of your hand. You hold my future, so I never have reason to fear. Through you I have the gift of eternal life, and your faithful guidance makes my life full.

ETERNAL LIFE

JOHN 3:16
God so loved the world that he gave his one and only Son, that whoever believes in him shall not perish but have eternal life.

1 JOHN 2:17
The world and its desires pass away, but the man who does the will of God lives forever.

ROMANS 6:23
The gift of God is eternal life in Christ Jesus our LORD.

JOHN 3:36
Whoever believes in the Son has eternal life.

JOHN 17:3
This is eternal life: that they may know you, the only true God, and Jesus Christ, whom you have sent.

HEBREWS 5:9
Once made perfect, Jesus became the source of eternal salvation for all who obey him.

PSALM 62:1–2
My soul finds rest in God alone;
    my salvation comes from him.
He alone is my rock and my salvation;
    he is my fortress, I will never be shaken.

1 JOHN 5:11–12
God has given us eternal life, and this life is in his
Son. He who has the Son has life.

JOHN 10:27–29
Jesus said, "My sheep listen to my voice; I know
them, and they follow me. I give them eternal life,
and they shall never perish; no one can snatch them
out of my hand. My Father, who has given them to
me, is greater than all; no one can snatch them out of
my Father's hand."

JOHN 11:25–26
Jesus said, "I am the resurrection and the life. He who
believes in me will live, even though he dies; and
whoever lives and believes in me will never die."

ROMANS 10:9–10

If you confess with your mouth, "Jesus is LORD," and believe in your heart that God raised him from the dead, you will be saved. For it is with your heart that you believe and are justified, and it is with your mouth that you confess and are saved.

HEBREWS 9:28

Christ was sacrificed once to take away the sins of many people; and he will appear a second time, not to bear sin, but to bring salvation to those who are waiting for him.

JOHN 14:2–3

Jesus said, "In my Father's house are many rooms ... I am going there to prepare a place for you. And if I go and prepare a place for you, I will come back and take you to be with me that you also may be where I am."

2 CORINTHIANS 5:1

We know that if the earthly tent we live in is destroyed, we have a building from God, an eternal house in heaven, not built by human hands.

ETERNAL LIFE

JOHN 6:47
He who believes has everlasting life.

REVELATION 21:1, 3–4
I saw a new heaven and a new earth, for the first
heaven and the first earth had passed away, and there
was no longer any sea.... And I heard a loud voice
from the throne saying, "Now the dwelling of God is
with men, and he will live with them. They will be his
people, and God himself will be with them and be
their God. He will wipe every tear from their eyes.
There will be no more death or mourning or crying or
pain, for the old order of things has passed away."

REVELATION 7:16–17
"Never again will they hunger;
    never again will they thirst.
The sun will not beat upon them,
    nor any scorching heat.
For the Lamb at the center of the throne will be their
shepherd;
    he will lead them to springs of living water.
And God will wipe away every tear from their eyes."

ACTS 3:19

Repent, then, and turn to God, so that your sins may
be wiped out, that times of refreshing may come from
the LORD.

2 PETER 3:9

The LORD is not slow in keeping his promise, as some
understand slowness. He is patient with you, not
wanting anyone to perish, but everyone to come
to repentance.

REVELATION 21:27

Nothing impure will ever enter the Holy City, ... but
only those whose names are written in the Lamb's
book of life.

TITUS 3:4–7

When the kindness and love of God our Savior
appeared, he saved us, not because of righteous
things we had done, but because of his mercy. He
saved us through the washing of rebirth and renewal
by the Holy Spirit, whom he poured out on us generously through Jesus Christ our Savior, so that, having
been justified by his grace, we might become heirs
having the hope of eternal life.

ETERNAL LIFE

JOHN 6:37-40
Jesus declared, "All that the Father gives me will come to me, and whoever comes to me I will never drive away. For I have come down from heaven not to do my will but to do the will of him who sent me. And this is the will of him who sent me, that I shall lose none of all that he has given me, but raise them up at the last day. For my Father's will is that everyone who looks to the Son and believes in him shall have eternal life, and I will raise him up at the last day."

JUDE 1:21
Keep yourselves in God's love as you wait for the mercy of our LORD Jesus Christ to bring you to eternal life.

REVELATION 22:14
"Blessed are those who wash their robes, that they may have the right to the tree of life and may go through the gates into the city."

LUKE 10:20
Rejoice that your names are written in heaven.

A FULL LIFE ON EARTH

JOHN 10:10
Jesus said, "I have come that [those who believe] may have life, and have it to the full."

DEUTERONOMY 30:20
Love the LORD your God, listen to his voice, and hold fast to him. For the LORD is your life.

JOHN 6:35
Jesus declared, "I am the bread of life. He who comes to me will never go hungry, and he who believes in me will never be thirsty."

2 CORINTHIANS 3:17
The LORD is the Spirit, and where the Spirit of the LORD is, there is freedom.

ROMANS 6:11
Count yourselves dead to sin but alive to God in Christ Jesus.

ROMANS 8:2
Through Christ Jesus the law of the Spirit of life set me free from the law of sin and death.

JOHN 6:63

Jesus said, "The Spirit gives life; the flesh counts for nothing. The words I have spoken to you are spirit and they are life."

ROMANS 8:11

If the Spirit of God who raised Jesus from the dead is living in you, he who raised Christ from the dead will also give life to your mortal bodies through his Spirit, who lives in you.

JOB 33:4

The Spirit of God has made me;
the breath of the Almighty gives me life.

PROVERBS 3:1–2

Do not forget my teaching,
but keep my commands in your heart,
for they will prolong your life many years
and bring you prosperity.

LUKE 17:21
Jesus said, "The kingdom of God is within you."

ROMANS 14:17
The kingdom of God is not a matter of eating and drinking, but of righteousness, peace and joy in the Holy Spirit.

LUKE 12:32
Jesus said to his disciples, "Do not be afraid, little flock, for your Father has been pleased to give you the kingdom."

DEUTERONOMY 5:33
Walk in all the way that the LORD your God has commanded you, so that you may live and prosper and prolong your days in the land that you will possess.

1 TIMOTHY 6:11–12
Pursue righteousness, godliness, faith, love, endurance and gentleness. Fight the good fight of the faith. Take hold of the eternal life to which you were called when you made your good confession in the presence of many witnesses.

A FULL LIFE ON EARTH

ISAIAH 30:21

Whether you turn to the right or to the left, your ears will hear a voice behind you, saying, "This is the way; walk in it."

PSALM 36:7–10

How priceless is your unfailing love, O LORD!
Both high and low among men
find refuge in the shadow of your wings.
They feast on the abundance of your house;
you give them drink from your river of delights.
For with you is the fountain of life;
in your light we see light.

Continue your love to those who know you,
your righteousness to the upright in heart.

PLANS FOR THE FUTURE

JEREMIAH 29:11-13

"I know the plans I have for you," declares the LORD, "plans to prosper you and not to harm you, plans to give you hope and a future. Then you will call upon me and come and pray to me, and I will listen to you. You will seek me and find me when you seek me with all your heart."

1 CORINTHIANS 2:9-10

As it is written:

"No eye has seen,
    no ear has heard,
no mind has conceived
    what God has prepared
    for those who love him"—

but God has revealed it to us by his Spirit. The Spirit searches all things, even the deep things of God.

PSALM 37:4

Delight yourself in the LORD
    and he will give you the desires of your heart.

1 CORINTHIANS 15:58

Stand firm. Let nothing move you. Always give yourselves fully to the work of the LORD, because you
know that your labor in the LORD is not in vain.

PSALM 138:8

The LORD will fulfill his purpose for me;
    your love, O LORD, endures forever—
    do not abandon the works of your hands.

1 JOHN 3:2

Dear friends, now we are children of God, and what
we will be has not yet been made known. But we
know that when he appears, we shall be like him, for
we shall see him as he is.

PSALM 33:11

The plans of the LORD stand firm forever,
    the purposes of his heart through all generations.

JOHN 16:33

Jesus said, "I have told you these things, so that in me you may have peace. In this world you will have trouble. But take heart! I have overcome the world."

MATTHEW 6:33–34

Jesus said to his disciples, "Seek first God's kingdom and his righteousness, and all these things will be given to you as well. Therefore do not worry about tomorrow, for tomorrow will worry about itself. Each day has enough trouble of its own."

ISAIAH 43:18–19

"Forget the former things;
    do not dwell on the past.
See, I am doing a new thing!
    Now it springs up; do you not perceive it?
I am making a way in the desert
    and streams in the wasteland,"
        says the LORD.

EZEKIEL 36:26

God said, "I will give you a new heart and put a new spirit in you; I will remove from you your heart of stone and give you a heart of flesh."

PLANS FOR THE FUTURE

MALACHI 3:10
"Bring the whole tithe into the storehouse, that there may be food in my house. Test me in this," says the LORD Almighty, "and see if I will not throw open the floodgates of heaven and pour out so much blessing that you will not have room enough for it."

ZECHARIAH 4:6
"Not by might nor by power, but by my Spirit," says the LORD Almighty.

PSALM 20:4
May the LORD give you the desire of your heart
    and make all your plans succeed.

JOSHUA 1:7
God said, "Be strong and very courageous. Be careful to obey all the law my servant Moses gave you; do not turn from it to the right or to the left, that you may be successful wherever you go."

PROVERBS 13:4
The desires of the diligent are fully satisfied.

PROVERBS 16:9

In his heart a man plans his course,
    but the LORD determines his steps.

MATTHEW 6:20–21

Jesus said to his disciples, "Store up for yourselves treasures in heaven, where moth and rust do not destroy, and where thieves do not break in and steal. For where your treasure is, there your heart will be also."

PSALM 1:1–3

Blessed is the man
    who does not walk in the counsel of the wicked
or stand in the way of sinners
    or sit in the seat of mockers.
His delight is in the law of the LORD,
    and on his law he meditates day and night.
He is like a tree planted by streams of water,
    which yields its fruit in season
and whose leaf does not wither.
    Whatever he does prospers.

PLANS FOR THE FUTURE

PROVERBS 16:1, 3
To man belong the plans of the heart,
    but from the LORD comes the reply of the tongue.

Commit to the LORD whatever you do,
    and your plans will succeed.

PROVERBS 3:5–6
Trust in the LORD with all your heart
    and lean not on your own understanding;
in all your ways acknowledge him,
    and he will make your paths straight.

WAIT FOR GOD AND HE WILL PROVIDE

LAMENTATIONS 3:24
The LORD is my portion;
therefore I will wait for him.

PSALM 5:3
In the morning, O LORD, you hear my voice;
in the morning I lay my requests before you
and wait in expectation.

ROMANS 2:7
To those who by persistence in doing good seek glory,
honor and immortatlity, he will give eternal life.

PSALM 27:14
Wait for the LORD;
be strong and take heart
and wait for the LORD.

ISAIAH 30:18
The LORD longs to be gracious to you;
    he rises to show you compassion.
For the LORD is a God of justice.
    Blessed are all who wait for him!

PSALM 33:20
We wait in hope for the LORD;
    he is our help and our shield.

ROMANS 8:25
If we hope for what we do not yet have, we wait for
it patiently.

PSALM 38:15
I wait for you, O LORD;
    you will answer, O Lord my God.

PSALM 119:166
I wait for your salvation, O LORD,
    and I follow your commands.

PSALM 130:5-6

I wait for the LORD, my soul waits,
 and in his word I put my hope.
My soul waits for the LORD
 more than watchmen wait for the morning.

ISAIAH 26:8

Yes, LORD, walking in the way of your laws,
 we wait for you;
your name and renown
 are the desire of our hearts.

ISAIAH 51:5

"My righteousness draws near speedily,
 my salvation is on the way,
 and my arm will bring justice to the nations.
The islands will look to me
 and wait in hope for my arm."
 declares the LORD.

WAIT FOR GOD AND HE WILL PROVIDE

1 CORINTHIANS 1:7

You do not lack any spiritual gift as you eagerly wait for our LORD Jesus Christ to be revealed.

ISAIAH 64:4

Since ancient times no one has heard,
   no ear has perceived,
no eye has seen any God besides you,
   who acts on behalf of those who wait for him.

MICAH 7:7

I watch in hope for the LORD,
   I wait for God my Savior;
   my God will hear me.

1 CORINTHIANS 4:5

Judge nothing before the appointed time; wait till the LORD comes. He will bring to light what is hidden in darkness and will expose the motives of men's hearts. At that time each will receive his praise from God.

JUDE 1:21

Keep yourselves in God's love as you wait for the mercy of our LORD Jesus Christ to bring you to eternal life.

JOHN 16:33

Jesus said, "I have told you these things, so that in me you may have peace. In this world you will have trouble. But take heart! I have overcome the world."

PSALM 60:12

With God we will gain the victory,
    and he will trample down our enemies.

HOSEA 6:3

Let us acknowledge the LORD;
    let us press on to acknowledge him.
As surely as the sun rises,
    he will appear;
he will come to us like the winter rains,
    like the spring rains that water the earth.

WAIT FOR GOD AND HE WILL PROVIDE

PSALM 40:1-2

I waited patiently for the LORD;
  he turned to me and heard my cry.
He lifted me out of the slimy pit,
  out of the mud and mire;
he set my feet on a rock
  and gave me a firm place to stand.

JOEL 2:23

Be glad, O people of Zion,
  rejoice in the LORD your God,
for he has given you
  the autumn rains in righteousness.
He sends you abundant showers,
  both autumn and spring rains, as before.

GOD HEARS YOUR PRAYERS

JEREMIAH 29:12
"You will call upon me and come and pray to me, and
I will listen to you," declares the LORD.

PSALM 66:19–20
God has surely listened
    and heard my voice in prayer.
Praise be to God,
    who has not rejected my prayer
    or withheld his love from me!

2 CHRONICLES 6:40
"Now, my God, may your eyes be open and your ears
attentive to the prayers offered in this place."

PSALM 34:17
    The righteous cry out, and the LORD hears them;
        he delivers them from all their troubles.

PSALM 69:33
The LORD hears the needy
    and does not despise his captive people.

HEBREWS 5:7
During the days of Jesus' life on earth, he offered up
prayers and petitions with loud cries and tears to the
one who could save him from death, and he was
heard because of his reverent submission.

2 CHRONICLES 7:14
God said, "If my people, who are called by my name, will
humble themselves and pray and seek my face and turn
from their wicked ways, then will I hear from heaven and
will forgive their sin and will heal their land."

PSALM 65:2
O you, LORD, who hear prayer,
    to you all men will come.

PROVERBS 15:29
God hears the prayer of the righteous.

PROVERBS 15:8
The prayer of the upright pleases God.

ROMANS 8:26
The Spirit helps us in our weakness. We do not know what we ought to pray for, but the Spirit himself intercedes for us with groans that words cannot express.

PHILIPPIANS 4:6–7
Do not be anxious about anything, but in everything, by prayer and petition, with thanksgiving, present your requests to God. And the peace of God, which transcends all understanding, will guard your hearts and your minds in Christ Jesus.

JAMES 5:13
Is any one of you in trouble? He should pray. Is anyone happy? Let him sing songs of praise.

1 PETER 3:12
The eyes of the LORD are on the righteous
        and his ears are attentive to their prayer.

GOD HEARS YOUR PRAYERS

PSALM 4:3
The LORD will hear when I call to him.

JOHN 15:7
Jesus said, "If you remain in me and my words remain in you, ask whatever you wish, and it will be given you."

MATTHEW 18:19
Jesus said to his disciples, "I tell you that if two of you on earth agree about anything you ask for, it will be done for you by my Father in heaven."

PSALM 31:22
In my alarm I said,
    "I am cut off from your sight!"
Yet you heard my cry for mercy, O LORD,
    when I called to you for help.

GOD ANSWERS YOUR PRAYERS

JAMES 5:15–16
The prayer offered in faith will make the sick person well; the LORD will raise him up. If he has sinned, he will be forgiven. Therefore confess your sins to each other and pray for each other so that you may be healed. The prayer of a righteous man is powerful and effective.

MATTHEW 21:22
Jesus said to his disciples, "If you believe, you will receive whatever you ask for in prayer."

JEREMIAH 31:9
"My people will come with weeping;
     they will pray as I bring them back.
I will lead them beside streams of water
     on a level path where they will not stumble.

PSALM 102:17
The LORD will respond to the prayer of the destitute;
     he will not despise their plea.

PSALM 6:9
The LORD has heard my cry for mercy;
the LORD accepts my prayer.

PSALM 17:6
I call on you, O God, for you will answer me;
give ear to me and hear my prayer.

DEUTERONOMY 4:7
The LORD our God is near us whenever we pray to
him.

MATTHEW 17:20
Jesus said, "If you have faith as small as a mustard
seed, you can say to this mountain, 'Move from here
to there' and it will move. Nothing will be impossible
for you."

MARK 11:24
Jesus said, "Whatever you ask for in prayer, believe
that you have received it, and it will be yours."

2 CHRONICLES 32:24

Hezekiah became ill and was at the point of death. He prayed to the LORD, who answered him and gave him a miraculous sign.

DANIEL 9:23

The angel Gabriel said to Daniel, "As soon as you began to pray, an answer was given, which I have come to tell you, for you are highly esteemed."

MATTHEW 7:7-8

Jesus said to his disciples, "As and it will be given to you; seek and you will find; knock and the door will be opened to you. For everyone who asks receives; he who seeks finds; and to him who knocks, the door will be opened."

PSALM 91:15

He will call upon me, and I will answer him;
    I will be with him in trouble,
    I will deliver him and honor him,"
        declares the LORD.

GOD ANSWERS YOUR PRAYERS

JAMES 5:17-18

Elijah was a man just like us. He prayed earnestly that it would not rain, and it did not rain on the land for three and a half years. Again he prayed, and the heavens gave rain, and the earth produced its crops.

ACTS 12:5-7, 9-11

Peter was kept in prison, but the church was earnestly praying to God for him. The night before Herod was to bring him to trial, Peter was sleeping between two soldiers, bound with two chains, and sentries stood guard at the entrance. Suddenly an angel of the LORD appeared and a light shone in the cell. He struck Peter on the side and woke him up. "Quick, get up!" he said, and the chains fell off Peter's wrists.... Peter followed [the angel] out of the prison, but he had no idea that what the angel was doing was really happening; he thought he was seeing a vision. They passed the first and second guards and came to the iron gate leading to the city. It opened for them by itself, and they went through it. When they had walked the length of one street, suddenly the angel left him. Then Peter came to himself and said, "Now I know without a doubt that the LORD sent his angel and rescued me...."

FINDING GOD'S WILL

JEREMIAH 29:13
"You will seek me and find me when you seek me with all your heart," declares the LORD.

ROMANS 12:2
Do not conform any longer to the pattern of this world, but be transformed by the renewing of your mind. Then you will be able to test and approve what God's will is—his good, pleasing and perfect will.

COLOSSIANS 1:9
Since the day we heard about you, we have not stopped praying for you and asking God to fill you with the knowledge of his will through all spiritual wisdom and understanding.

1 THESSALONIANS 5:18
Give thanks in all circumstances, for this is God's will for you in Christ Jesus.

1 PETER 2:15
It is God's will that by doing good you should silence the ignorant talk of foolish men.

MARK 3:35
Jesus said, "Whoever does God's will is my brother and sister and mother."

JOHN 9:31
God listens to the godly man who does his will.

EPHESIANS 1:9
God made known to us the mystery of his will according to his good pleasure, which he purposed in Christ.

EPHESIANS 1:11
In Christ we were also chosen, having been predestined according to the plan of God who works out everything in conformity with the purpose of his will.

1 JOHN 5:14
This is the confidence we have in approaching God: that if we ask anything according to his will, he hears us.

JEREMIAH 6:16

This is what the LORD says:
"Stand at the crossroads and look;
    ask for the ancient paths,
ask where the good way is, and walk in it,
    and you will find rest for your souls."

JAMES 1:5

If any of you lacks wisdom, he should ask God, who gives generously to all without finding fault, and it will be given to him.

JEREMIAH 33:3

"Call to me and I will answer you and tell you great and unsearchable things you do not know," says the LORD.

JOHN 14:16–17

Jesus said, "I will ask the Father, and he will give you another Counselor to be with you forever—the Spirit of truth. The world cannot accept him, because it neither sees him nor knows him. But you know him, for he lives with you and will be in you."

FINDING GOD'S WILL

PROVERBS 3:5-6
Trust in the LORD with all your heart
    and lean not on your own understanding;
in all your ways acknowledge him,
    and he will make your paths straight.

PROVERBS 16:9
In his heart a man plans his course,
    but the LORD determines his steps.

PSALM 37:23-24
If the LORD delights in a man's way,
    he makes his steps firm;
though he stumble, he will not fall,
    for the LORD upholds him with his hand.

PSALM 37:4
Delight yourself in the LORD
    and he will give you the desires of your heart.

PHILIPPIANS 3:13–14

One thing I do: Forgetting what is behind and straining toward what is ahead, I press on toward the goal to win the prize for which God has called me heavenward in Christ Jesus.

1 CORINTHIANS 2:16

"Who has known the mind of the Lord
    that he may instruct him?"

But we have the mind of Christ.

ROMANS 8:27–28

God who searches our hearts knows the mind of the Spirit, because the Spirit intercedes for the saints in accordance with God's will. And we know that in all things God works for the good of those who love him, who have been called according to his purpose.

EPHESIANS 1:9–10

God made known to us the mystery of his will according to his good pleasure, which he purposed in Christ, to be put into effect when the times will have reached their fulfillment––to bring all things in heaven and on earth together under one head, even Christ.

FINDING GOD'S WILL

1 PETER 4:19

Those who suffer according to God's will should commit themselves to their faithful Creator and continue to do good.

1 THESSALONIANS 4:3

It is God's will that you should be sanctified.

1 JOHN 2:17

The world and its desires pass away, but the man who does the will of God lives forever.

CHAPTER

4

WHAT DOES GOD PROVIDE IN TIMES OF NEED?

Promises about the Fruit of the Spirit

Thank you, LORD Jesus, for your generous provision. Thank you that when I invited you into my life, you made my heart your dwelling place. Because your Spirit lives within me, you empower me to bear the fruit of the Spirit.

LOVE

1 CORINTHIANS 13:4–6

Love is patient, love is kind. It does not envy, it does not boast, it is not proud. It is not rude, it is not self-seeking, it is not easily angered, it keeps no record of wrongs. Love does not delight in evil but rejoices with the truth.

2 TIMOTHY 1:7

God did not give us a spirit of timidity, but a spirit of power, of love and of self-discipline.

1 PETER 4:8

Above all, love each other deeply, because love covers over a multitude of sins.

1 JOHN 4:19

We love because God first loved us.

EPHESIANS 5:2

Live a life of love, just as Christ loved us and gave himself up for us as a fragrant offering and sacrifice to God.

LUKE 6:35

Jesus said, "Love your enemies, do good to them, and lend to them without expecting to get anything back. Then your reward will be great, and you will be sons of the Most High."

JOHN 13:34–35

Jesus said, "Love one another. As I have loved you, so you must love one another. By this all men will know that you are my disciples, if you love one another."

JOHN 14:21

Jesus said, "Whoever has my commands and obeys them, he is the one who loves me. He who loves me will be loved by my Father, and I too will love him and show myself to him."

ROMANS 8:28

We know that in all things God works for the good of those who love him, who have been called according to his purpose.

1 CORINTHIANS 13:8

Love never fails.

1 CORINTHIANS 13:13

These three remain: faith, hope and love. But the greatest of these is love.

EPHESIANS 3:17–19

I pray that you, being rooted and established in love, may have power, together with all the saints, to grasp how wide and long and high and deep is the love of Christ, and to know this love that surpasses knowledge—that you may be filled to the measure of all the fullness of God.

EPHESIANS 6:24

Grace to all who love our LORD Jesus Christ with an undying love.

1 THESSALONIANS 3:12

May the LORD make your love increase and overflow for each other and for everyone else.

1 PETER 1:22

Now that you have purified yourselves by obeying the truth so that you have sincere love for your brothers, love one another deeply, from the heart.

LOVE

HEBREWS 10:24
Let us consider how we may spur one another on
toward love and good deeds.

1 JOHN 4:7
Dear friends, let us love one another, for love comes
from God. Everyone who loves has been born of God
and knows God.

ROMANS 13:8
Let no debt remain outstanding, except the continuing
debt to love one another, for he who loves his fellowman
has fulfilled the law.

PROVERBS 17:9
He who covers over an offense promotes love,
    but whoever repeats the matter separates close friends.

1 JOHN 4:16
We know and rely on the love God has for us. God is
love. Whoever lives in love lives in God, and God in him.

DEUTERONOMY 33:12

Let the beloved of the LORD rest secure in him,
  for he shields him all day long,
    and the one the LORD loves rests between
      his shoulders.

PSALM 23:6

Surely goodness and love will follow me
  all the days of my life,
and I will dwell in the house of the LORD forever.

DEUTERONOMY 33:3

Surely it is you, LORD, who love the people;
  all the holy ones are in your hand.
At your feet they all bow down,
  and from you receive instruction.

1 PETER 3:8

Live in harmony with one another; be sympathetic,
love as brothers, be compassionate and humble.

MATTHEW 22:37

Jesus replied, "Love the LORD your God with all your heart and with all your sould and with all your mind."

JOHN 14:23

Jesus replied, "If anyone love me, he will obey my teaching. My Father will love him, and we will come to him and make our home with him."

MATTHEW 5:44–45

Jesus said, "Love your enemies and pray for those who persecute you, that you may be sons of your Father in heaven."

JOY

NEHEMIAH 8:10
The joy of the LORD is your strength.

JOB 8:21
God will yet fill your mouth with laughter
    and your lips with shouts of joy.

ISAIAH 55:12
You will go out in joy
    and be led forth in peace;
the mountains and hills
    will burst into song before you,
and all the trees of the field
    will clap their hands.

PSALM 97:11
Light is shed upon the righteous
    and joy on the upright in heart.

PSALM 63:3–5
Because your love is better than life, O LORD,
    my lips will glorify you.
I will praise you as long as I live,
    and in your name I will lift up my hands.
My soul will be satisfied as with the richest of
        foods;
    with singing lips my mouth will praise you.

PSALM 119:111
Your statutes are my heritage forever, O LORD;
    they are the joy of my heart.

PROVERBS 15:30
A cheerful look brings joy to the heart,
    and good news gives health to the bones.

PSALM 92:4
You make me glad by your deeds, O LORD;
    I sing for joy at the works of your hands.

ISAIAH 51:11
The ransomed of the LORD will return.
    They will enter Zion with singing;
    everlasting joy will crown their heads.
Gladness and joy will overtake them,
    and sorrow and sighing will flee away.

HEBREWS 1:9
You have loved righteousness and hated wickedness;
    therefore God, your God, has set you above
    your companions
    by anointing you with the oil of joy.

PSALM 19:8
The precepts of the LORD are right,
    giving joy to the heart.
The commands of the LORD are radiant,
    giving light to the eyes.

LUKE 6:22–23
Blessed are you when men hate you,
    when they exclude you and insult you
    and reject your name as evil,
        because of the Son of Man.
Rejoice in that day and leap for joy, because great is
your reward in heaven. For that is how their fathers
treated the prophets.

PSALM 30:11–12
You turned my wailing into dancing;
    you removed my sackcloth and clothed me with joy,
that my heart may sing to you and not be silent.
    O LORD my God, I will give you thanks forever.

PSALM 5:11
Let all who take refuge in you be glad, O LORD;
    let them ever sing for joy.

1 PETER 1:8–9

Though you have not seen Jesus, you love him; and even though you do not see him now, you believe in him and are filled with an inexpressible and glorious joy, for you are receiving the goal of your faith, the salvation of your souls.

PSALM 16:11

You have made known to me the path of life,
> O LORD;
>> you will fill me with joy in your presence,
>> with eternal pleasures at your right hand.

JOHN 16:24

Jesus said, "Until now you have not asked for anything in my name. Ask and you will receive, and your joy will be complete."

PSALM 13:5–6

I trust in your unfailing love, O LORD;
> my heart rejoices in your salvation.
I will sing to the LORD,
> for he has been good to me.

JOY

JOB 33:26, 28
[A person] prays to God and finds favor with him,
he sees God's face and shouts for joy;
he is restored by God to his righteous state....
Then he ... says,
"God redeemed my soul from going down to the pit,
and I will live to enjoy the light."

ACTS 2:26-28
Therefore my heart is glad and my tongue rejoices;
my body also will live in hope,
because you will not abandon me to the grave,
nor will you let your Holy One see decay.
You have made known to me the paths of life;
you will fill me with joy in your presence.

PATIENCE AND PERSEVERANCE

PSALM 40:1
I waited patiently for the LORD;
> he turned to me and heard my cry.

PSALM 37:7
Be still before the LORD and wait patiently for him.

PROVERBS 19:11
A man's wisdom gives him patience;
> it is to his glory to overlook an offense.

PROVERBS 12:16
A prudent man overlooks an insult.

PSALM 27:14
Wait for the LORD;
> be strong and take heart
> and wait for the LORD.

ECCLESIASTES 7:8
The end of a matter is better than its beginning,
    and patience is better than pride.

EPHESIANS 4:2
Be completely humble and gentle; be patient, bearing
with one another in love.

ROMANS 5:3–4
We also rejoice in our sufferings, because we know
that suffering produces perseverance; perseverance,
character; and character, hope.

JAMES 1:2–4
Consider it pure joy, my brothers, whenever you face
trials of many kinds, because you know that the testing of your faith develops perseverance. Perseverance
must finish its work so that you may be mature and
complete, not lacking anything.

ROMANS 8:25
If we hope for what we do not yet have, we wait for
it patiently.

COLOSSIANS 1:10–11

We pray ... that you may live a life worthy of the LORD and may please him in every way: bearing fruit in every good work, growing in the knowledge of God, being strengthened with all power according to his glorious might so that you may have great endurance and patience.

1 TIMOTHY 1:16

I was shown mercy so that in me, the worst of sinners, Christ Jesus might display his unlimited patience as an example for those who would believe on him and receive eternal life.

HEBREWS 10:36

You need to persevere so that when you have done the will of God, you will receive what he has promised.

JAMES 5:7–8

See how the farmer waits for the land to yield its valuable crop and how patient he is for the autumn and spring rains. You too, be patient and stand firm, because the LORD's coming is near.

PATIENCE AND PERSEVERANCE

GALATIANS 6:9
Let us not become weary in doing good, for at the proper time we will reap a harvest if we do not give up.

2 PETER 3:9
The LORD is not slow in keeping his promise, as some understand slowness. He is patient with you, not wanting anyone to perish, but everyone to come to repentance.

PSALM 130:5-6
I wait for the LORD, my soul waits,
    and in his word I put my hope.
My soul waits for the Lord
    more than watchmen wait for the morning.

JAMES 5:10-11
As an example of patience in the face of suffering, take the prophets who spoke in the name of the LORD. As you know, we consider blessed those who have persevered. You have heard of Job's perseverance and have seen what the LORD finally brought about. The LORD is full of compassion and mercy.

2 CORINTHIANS 1:6–7

If we are distressed, it is for your comfort and salvation; if we are comforted, it is for your comfort, which produces in you patient endurance of the same sufferings we suffer. And our hope for you is firm, because we know that just as you share in our sufferings, so also you share in our comfort.

REVELATION 3:10–12

Jesus says, "Since you have kept my command to endure patiently, I will also keep you from the hour of trial that is going to come upon the whole world to test those who live on the earth. I am coming soon. Hold on to what you have, so that no one will take your crown. Him who overcomes I will make a pillar in the temple of my God. Never again will he leave it. I will write on him the name of my God and the name of the city of my God, the new Jerusalem, which is coming down out of heaven from my God; and I will also write on him my new name."

PATIENCE AND PERSEVERANCE

PROVERBS 14:29
A patient man has great understanding.

ROMANS 12:12
Be joyful in hope, patient in affliction, faithful in prayer.

1 THESSALONIANS 5:14
We urge you, brothers, warn those who are idle, encourage
the timid, help the weak, be patient with everyone.

2 CORINTHIANS 4:17
Our light and momentary troubles are achieving for us
an eternal glory that far outweighs them all.

PEACE

ROMANS 8:6
The mind controlled by the Spirit is life and peace.

ISAIAH 26:3
You will keep in perfect peace
    him whose mind is steadfast,
    because he trusts in you, O LORD.

JOHN 14:27
Jesus said, "Peace I leave with you; my peace I give
you. I do not give to you as the world gives. Do not
let your hearts be troubled and do not be afraid."

ROMANS 5:1
Since we have been justified through faith, we have
peace with God through our LORD Jesus Christ.

PSALM 85:8
I will listen to what God the LORD will say;
    he promises peace to his people, his saints.

PSALM 29:11
The LORD gives strength to his people;
    the LORD blesses his people with peace.

MATTHEW 5:9
Blessed are the peacemakers,
    for they will be called sons of God.

2 CORINTHIANS 13:11
Aim for perfection, listen to my appeal, be of one
mind, live in peace. And the God of love and peace
will be with you.

PROVERBS 16:7
When a man's ways are pleasing to the LORD,
    he makes even his enemies live at peace with him.

PSALM 119:165
Great peace have they who love your law, O LORD,
    and nothing can make them stumble.

PSALM 4:8
I will lie down and sleep in peace,
    for you alone, O LORD,
    make me dwell in safety.

PSALM 23:1–4
The LORD is my shepherd, I shall not be in want.
    He makes me lie down in green pastures,
he leads me beside quiet waters,
    he restores my soul.
He guides me in paths of righteousness
    for his name's sake.
Even though I walk
    through the valley of the shadow of death,
I will fear no evil,
    for you are with me;
your rod and your staff,
    they comfort me.

PEACE

PHILIPPIANS 4:6–7
In everything, by prayer and petition, with thanksgiving, present your requests to God. And the peace of God, which transcends all understanding, will guard your hearts and your minds in Christ Jesus.

PSALM 62:1
My soul finds rest in God alone;
    my salvation comes from him.

PROVERBS 14:30
A heart at peace gives life to the body.

ISAIAH 26:12
LORD, you establish peace for us;
    all that we have accomplished you have done
        for us.

MATTHEW 11:28
Jesus said, "Come to me, all you who are weary and burdened, and I will give you rest."

EPHESIANS 2:17
Jesus came and preached peace to you who were far away and peace to those who were near.

JOHN 20:21
Jesus said, "Peace be with you! As the Father has sent me, I am sending you."

JAMES 3:17–18
The wisdom that comes from heaven is first of all pure; then peace-loving, considerate, submissive, full of mercy and good fruit, impartial and sincere. Peacemakers who sow in peace raise a harvest of righteousness.

1 PETER 5:7
Cast all your anxiety on God because he cares for you.

PSALM 37:37
Consider the blameless, observe the upright;
    there is a future for the man of peace.

PEACE

ROMANS 14:17–19
The kingdom of God is not a matter of eating and drinking, but of righteousness, peace and joy in the Holy Spirit, because anyone who serves Christ in this way is pleasing to God and approved by men. Let us therefore make every effort to do what leads to peace and to mutual edification.

2 PETER 1:2
Grace and peace be yours in abundance through the knowledge of God and of Jesus our LORD.

1 CORINTHIANS 14:33
God is not a God fo disorder, but of peace.

HOPE

LAMENTATIONS 3:21, 25–26
This I call to mind
    and therefore I have hope: ...
The LORD is good to those whose hope is in him,
    to the one who seeks him;
it is good to wait quietly
    for the salvation of the LORD.

PSALM 71:5
You have been my hope, O Sovereign LORD,
    my confidence since my youth.

ISAIAH 40:31
Those who hope in the LORD
    will renew their strength.
They will soar on wings like eagles;
    they will run and not grow weary,
    they will walk and not be faint.

1 PETER 1:3

Praise be to the God and Father of our LORD Jesus Christ! In his great mercy he has given us new birth into a living hope through the resurrection of Jesus Christ from the dead.

ROMANS 5:2-5

We rejoice in the hope of the glory of God. Not only so, but we also rejoice in our sufferings, because we know that suffering produces perseverance; perseverance, character; and character, hope. And hope does not disappoint us, because God has poured out his love into our hearts by the Holy Spirit, whom he has given us.

1 TIMOTHY 4:10

We have put our hope in the living God, who is the Savior of all men, and especially of those who believe.

1 PETER 1:21

Through Jesus you believe in God, who raised him from the dead and glorified him, and so your faith and hope are in God.

ACTS 2:26–27

My heart is glad and my tongue rejoices;
    my body also will live in hope,
because you will not abandon me to the grave,
    nor will you let your Holy One see decay.

PSALM 147:11

The LORD delights in those who fear him,
    who put their hope in his unfailing love.

PROVERBS 24:14

Know also that wisdom is sweet to your soul;
    if you find it, there is a future hope for you,
    and your hope will not be cut off.

ROMANS 15:13

May the God of hope fill you with all joy and peace
as you trust in him, so that you may overflow with
hope by the power of the Holy Spirit.

HOPE

PSALM 42:11
Why are you downcast, O my soul?
Why so disturbed within me?
Put your hope in God,
for I will yet praise him,
my Savior and my God.

2 THESSALONIANS 2:16–17
May our LORD Jesus Christ himself and God our
Father, who loved us and by his grace gave us eternal
encouragement and good hope, encourage your hearts
and strengthen you in every good deed and word.

HEBREWS 6:17–19
Because God wanted to make the unchanging nature
of his purpose very clear to the heirs of what was
promised, he confirmed it with an oath. God did this
so that, by two unchangeable things in which it is
impossible for God to lie, we who have fled to take
hold of the hope offered to us may be greatly encour-
aged. We have this hope as an anchor for the soul,
firm and secure.

PSALM 119:114
You are my refuge and my shield, O LORD;
    I have put my hope in your word.

1 PETER 1:13
Set your hope fully on the grace to be given you
when Jesus Christ is revealed.

1 JOHN 3:3
Everyone who has this hope in him purifies himself,
just as Christ is pure.

TITUS 3:4–7
When the kindness and love of God our Savior
appeared, he saved us, not because of righteous
things we had done, but because of his mercy. He
saved us through the washing of rebirth and renewal
by the Holy Spirit, whom he poured out on us generously through Jesus Christ our Savior, so that, having
been justified by his grace, we might become heirs
having the hope of eternal life.

HOPE

P SALM 146:5-6
Blessed is he whose help is the God of Jacob,
    whose hope is in the LORD his God,
the Maker of heaven and earth,
    the sea, and everything in them--
    the LORD, who remains faithful forever.

P SALM 33:18
The eyes of the LORD are on those who fear him,
    on those whose hope is in his unfailing love,
to deliver them from death
    and keep them alive in famine.

CHAPTER

5

HOW DO YOU BEGIN YOUR LIFE IN CHRIST?

Promises about Becoming a Christian

Thank you, God, for the privilege of being your child and the amazing gift of salvation. I want to please you with all my heart. Open my eyes to see the truth and open my mind to hear your words of encouragement as I walk down the path of discipleship.

BEING BORN AGAIN

ROMANS 10:9–11

If you confess with your mouth, "Jesus is LORD," and believe in your heart that God raised him from the dead, you will be saved. For it is with your heart that you believe and are justified, and it is with your mouth that you confess and are saved. As the Scripture says, "Anyone who trusts in him will never be put to shame."

JOHN 5:24

Jesus answered, "I tell you the truth, whoever hears my word and believes him who sent me has eternal life and will not be condemned; he has crossed over from death to life."

1 PETER 1:23

You have been born again, not of perishable seed, but of imperishable, through the living and enduring word of God.

1 JOHN 2:29

If you know that he is righteous, you know that everyone who does what is right has been born of him.

JOHN 3:3

In reply Jesus declared, "I tell you the truth, no one can see the kingdom of God unless he is born again."

2 CORINTHIANS 5:17
Therefore, if anyone is in Christ, he is a new creation;
the old has gone, the new has come!

EPHESIANS 2:8-10
It is by grace you have been saved, through faith—and
this not from yourselves, it is the gift of God—not by
works, so that no one can boast. For we are God's
workmanship, created in Christ Jesus to do good
works, which God prepared in advance for us to do.

1 JOHN 5:1-6
Everyone who believes that Jesus is the Christ is born
of God, and everyone who loves the father loves his
child as well. This is how we know that we love the
children of God: by loving God and carrying out his
commands. This is love for God: to obey his commands. And his commands are not burdensome, for
everyone born of God overcomes the world. This is the
victory that has overcome the world, even our faith.
Who is it that overcomes the world? Only he who
believes that Jesus is the Son of God.
This is the one who came by water and blood—Jesus
Christ. He did not come by water only, but by water
and blood. And it is the Spirit who testifies, because
the Spirit is the truth.

1 JOHN 5:11–12

God has given us eternal life, and this life is in his
Son. He who has the Son has life; he who does not
have the Son of God does not have life.

MATTHEW 10:32, 38–39

Jesus said to his disciples, "Whoever acknowledges me
before men, I will also acknowledge him before my
Father in heaven.… And anyone who does not take his
cross and follow me is not worthy of me. Whoever
finds his life will lose it, and whoever loses his life for
my sake will find it."

GALATIANS 2:20

I have been crucified with Christ and I no longer live,
but Christ lives in me. The life I live in the body, I live
by faith in the Son of God, who loved me and gave
himself for me.

EZEKIEL 36:26–27

"I will give you a new heart and put a new spirit in
you; I will remove from you your heart of stone and
give you a heart of flesh. And I will put my Spirit in
you and move you to follow my decrees and be careful to keep my laws," declares the Sovereign LORD.

BEING BORN AGAIN

ROMANS 6:6-8

For we know that our old self was crucified with him
so that the body of sin might be done away with,
that we should no longer be slaves to sin—because
anyone who has died has been freed from sin.
Now if we died with Christ, we believe that we will
also live with him.

EPHESIANS 4:22-24

You were taught, with regard to your former way of
life, to put off your old self, which is being corrupted
by its deceitful desires; to be made new in the atti-
tude of your minds; and to put on the new self, created to be like God in true righteousness and holiness.

GALATIANS 5:24-25

Those who belong to Christ Jesus have crucified the
sinful nature with its passions and desires. Since we
live by the Spirit, let us keep in step with the Spirit.

1 TIMOTHY 6:12

Fight the good fight of the faith. Take hold of the eternal life to which you were called when you made your
good confession in the presence of many witnesses.

THE SUFFICIENCY OF JESUS

HEBREWS 12:2
Let us fix our eyes on Jesus, the author and perfecter of our faith, who for the joy set before him endured the cross, scorning its shame, and sat down at the right hand of the throne of God.

JOHN 6:35
Then Jesus declared, "I am the bread of life. He who comes to me will never go hungry, and he who believes in me will never be thirsty."

JOHN 8:36
Jesus replied, "If the Son sets you free, you will be free indeed."

HEBREWS 13:5-6, 8
... be content with what you have, because God has said,

"Never will I leave you;
     never will I forsake you."

So we say with confidence,

"The LORD is my helper; I will not be afraid.
     What can man do to me?"

Jesus Christ is the same yesterday and today and forever.

PSALM 73:25–26
Whom have I in heaven but you?
    And earth has nothing I desire besides you.
My flesh and my heart may fail,
    but God is the strength of my heart
    and my portion forever.

JOHN 10:17–18
Jesus said, "The reason my Father loves me is that I lay down my life—only to take it up again. No one takes it from me, but I lay it down of my own accord. I have authority to lay it down and authority to take it up again. This command I received from my Father."

JOHN 1:29–30
The next day John saw Jesus coming toward him and said, "Look, the Lamb of God, who takes away the sin of the world! This is the one I meant when I said, 'A man who comes after me has surpassed me because he was before me.'"

REVELATION 1:17–18
When I saw him, I fell at his feet as though dead. Then he placed his right hand on me and said: "Do not be afraid. I am the First and the Last. I am the Living One; I was dead, and behold I am alive for ever and ever! And I hold the keys of death and Hades."

MATTHEW 28:18–20

Then Jesus came to them and said, "All authority in heaven and on earth has been given to me. Therefore go and make disciples of all nations, baptizing them in the name of the Father and of the Son and of the Holy Spirit, and teaching them to obey everything I have commanded you. And surely I am with you always, to the very end of the age."

1 CORINTHIANS 3:10–11

By the grace God has given me, I laid a foundation as an expert builder, and someone else is building on it. But each one should be careful how he builds. For no one can lay any foundation other than the one already laid, which is Jesus Christ.

COLOSSIANS 2:9–10

In Christ all the fullness of the Deity lives in bodily form, and you have been given fullness in Christ, who is the head over every power and authority.

1 TIMOTHY 2:5

For there is one God and one mediator between God and men, the man Christ Jesus.

THE SUFFICIENCY OF JESUS

2 CORINTHIANS 3:4–5

Such confidence as this is ours through Christ before God. Not that we are competent in ourselves to claim anything for ourselves, but our competence comes from God.

2 TIMOTHY 4:17–18

The LORD stood at my side and gave me strength, so that through me the message might be fully proclaimed and all the Gentiles might hear it. And I was delivered from the lion's mouth. The LORD will rescue me from every evil attack and will bring me safely to his heavenly kingdom. To him be glory for ever and ever. Amen.

PSALM 121:2–3

My help comes from the LORD,
    the Maker of heaven and earth.
He will not let your foot slip—
    he who watches over you will not slumber;

JOHN 1:3–4

Through him all things were made; without him nothing was made that has been made. In him was life, and that life was the light of men.

BLOOD OF JESUS

MATTHEW 26:27-28

He took the cup, gave thanks and offered it to them, saying, "Drink from it, all of you. This is my blood of the covenant, which is poured out for many for the forgiveness of sins."

COLOSSIANS 1:19-22

God was pleased to have all his fullness dwell in him, and through him to reconcile to himself all things, whether things on earth or things in heaven, by making peace through his blood, shed on the cross. Once you were alienated from God and were enemies in your minds because of your evil behavior. But now he has reconciled you by Christ's physical body through death to present you holy in his sight, without blemish and free from accusation.

ROMANS 5:8-10

God demonstrates his own love for us in this: While we were still sinners, Christ died for us. Since we have now been justified by his blood, how much more shall we be saved from God's wrath through him! For if, when we were God's enemies, we were reconciled to him through the death of his Son, how much more, having been reconciled, shall we be saved through his life!

1 PETER 1:18-19, 21

You know that it was not with perishable things such as silver or gold that you were redeemed from the empty way of life handed down to you from your forefathers, but with the precious blood of Christ, a lamb without blemish or defect.... Through him you believe in God, who raised him from the dead and glorified him, and so your faith and hope are in God.

ROMANS 3:23-26

All have sinned and fall short of the glory of God, and are justified freely by his grace through the redemption that came by Christ Jesus. God presented him as a sacrifice of atonement, through faith in his blood. He did this to demonstrate his justice, because in his forbearance he had left the sins committed beforehand unpunished—he did it to demonstrate his justice at the present time, so as to be just and the one who justifies those who have faith in Jesus.

HEBREWS 9:14

How much more, then, will the blood of Christ, who through the eternal Spirit offered himself unblemished to God, cleanse our consciences from acts that lead to death, so that we may serve the living God!

EPHESIANS 2:13, 17–19

In Christ Jesus you who once were far away have been brought near through the blood of Christ.... He came and preached peace to you who were far away and peace to those who were near. For through him we both have access to the Father by one Spirit. Consequently, you are no longer foreigners and aliens, but fellow citizens with God's people and members of God's household.

LUKE 22:19–20

Jesus took bread, gave thanks and broke it, and gave it to them, saying, "This is my body given for you; do this in remembrance of me."
In the same way, after the supper he took the cup, saying, "This cup is the new covenant in my blood, which is poured out for you.

JOHN 6:53–54, 56

Jesus said to them, "I tell you the truth, unless you eat the flesh of the Son of Man and drink his blood, you have no life in you. Whoever eats my flesh and drinks my blood has eternal life, and I will raise him up at the last day.... Whoever eats my flesh and drinks my blood remains in me, and I in him.

BLOOD OF JESUS

LEVITICUS 17:11
The life of a creature is in the blood, and I have given it to you to make atonement for yourselves on the altar; it is the blood that makes atonement for one's life.

1 JOHN 1:7
If we walk in the light, as he is in the light, we have fellowship with one another, and the blood of Jesus, his Son, purifies us from all sin.

HEBREWS 10:19-20
We have confidence to enter the Most Holy Place by the blood of Jesus, by a new and living way opened for us through the curtain, that is, his body.

REVELATION 1:5-6
To him who loves us and has freed us from our sins by his blood, and has made us to be a kingdom and priests to serve his God and Father--to him be glory and power for ever and ever!

HEBREWS 9:22
The law requires that nearly everything be cleansed with blood, and without the shedding of blood there is no forgiveness.

REVELATION 5:9
They sang a new song:

"You are worthy to take the scroll
    and to open its seals,
because you were slain,
    and with your blood you purchased men for God
    from every tribe and language and people
        and nation.
You have made them to be a kingdom and priests to
        serve our God,
    and they will reign on the earth."

ACTS 20:28
Keep watch over yourselves and all the flock of which
the Holy Spirit has made you overseers. Be shepherds of
the church of God, which he bought with his own blood.

1 JOHN 5:6
This is the one who came by water and blood—Jesus Christ. He did not come by water only, but by water and blood. And it is the Spirit who testifies, because the Spirit is the truth.

HEBREWS 9:12
He did not enter by means of the blood of goats and calves; but he entered the Most Holy Place once for all by his own blood, having obtained eternal redemption.

POWER OF THE WORD

HEBREWS 4:12
The word of God is living and active. Sharper than any double-edged sword, it penetrates even to dividing soul and spirit, joints and marrow; it judges the thoughts and attitudes of the heart.

PSALM 119:11–16
I have hidden your word in my heart
    that I might not sin against you.
Praise be to you, O LORD;
    teach me your decrees.
With my lips I recount
    all the laws that come from your mouth.
I rejoice in following your statutes
    as one rejoices in great riches.
I meditate on your precepts
    and consider your ways.
I delight in your decrees;
    I will not neglect your word.

PSALM 119:103–105

How sweet are your words to my taste,
    sweeter than honey to my mouth!
I gain understanding from your precepts;
    therefore I hate every wrong path.
Your word is a lamp to my feet
    and a light for my path.

LUKE 21:33

Jesus said to his disciples, "Heaven and earth will pass away, but my words will never pass away."

JOHN 6:63–64

Jesus said to his disciples, "The Spirit gives life; the flesh counts for nothing. The words I have spoken to you are spirit and they are life. Yet there are some of you who do not believe."

JOHN 1:1–4

In the beginning was the Word, and the Word was with God, and the Word was God. He was with God in the beginning.

Through him all things were made; without him nothing was made that has been made. In him was life, and that life was the light of men.

PSALM 107:20-21

He sent forth his word and healed them;
  he rescued them from the grave.
Let them give thanks to the LORD for his unfailing love
  and his wonderful deeds for men.

2 TIMOTHY 3:15-17

From infancy you have known the holy Scriptures,
which are able to make you wise for salvation through
faith in Christ Jesus. All Scripture is God-breathed and
is useful for teaching, rebuking, correcting and train-
ing in righteousness, so that the man of God may be
thoroughly equipped for every good work.

PSALM 119:89-90

Your word, O LORD, is eternal;
  it stands firm in the heavens.
Your faithfulness continues through all generations;
  you established the earth, and it endures.

PSALM 33:6

By the word of the LORD were the heavens made,
  their starry host by the breath of his mouth.

POWER OF THE WORD

1 PETER 1:23–25

You have been born again, not of perishable seed, but of imperishable, through the living and enduring word of God. For,

> "All men are like grass,
>> and all their glory is like the flowers of the field;
> the grass withers and the flowers fall,
>> but the word of the LORD stands forever."

And this is the word that was preached to you.

JOHN 15:3

Jesus said, "You are already clean because of the word I have spoken to you."

MATTHEW 4:4

Jesus answered, "It is written: 'Man does not live on bread alone, but on every word that comes from the mouth of God.'"

WORK OF THE HOLY SPIRIT

1 CORINTHIANS 2:9–14

As it is written:

> "No eye has seen,
>   no ear has heard,
> no mind has conceived
> what God has prepared for those who love him"—

but God has revealed it to us by his Spirit.
The Spirit searches all things, even the deep things of God.
For who among men knows the thoughts of a man except
the man's spirit within him? In the same way no one
knows the thoughts of God except the Spirit of God. We
have not received the spirit of the world but the Spirit who
is from God, that we may understand what God has freely
given us. This is what we speak, not in words taught us by
human wisdom but in words taught by the Spirit, expressing spiritual truths in spiritual words. The man without the
Spirit does not accept the things that come from the Spirit
of God, for they are foolishness to him, and he cannot
understand them, because they are spiritually discerned.

LUKE 12:11–12

Jesus said to his disciples, "When you are brought before
synagogues, rulers and authorities, do not worry about how
you will defend yourselves or what you will say, for the Holy
Spirit will teach you at that time what you should say."

GALATIANS 5:22-25

The fruit of the Spirit is love, joy, peace, patience, kindness, goodness, faithfulness, gentleness and self-control. Against such things there is no law. Those who belong to Christ Jesus have crucified the sinful nature with its passions and desires. Since we live by the Spirit, let us keep in step with the Spirit.

JOHN 14:16-17, 26

Jesus said, "I will ask the Father, and he will give you another Counselor to be with you forever—the Spirit of truth. The world cannot accept him, because it neither sees him nor knows him. But you know him, for he lives with you and will be in you. The Counselor, the Holy Spirit, whom the Father will send in my name, will teach you all things and will remind you of everything I have said to you."

1 THESSALONIANS 1:5-6

Our gospel came to you not simply with words, but also with power, with the Holy Spirit and with deep conviction. You know how we lived among you for your sake. You became imitators of us and of the LORD; in spite of severe suffering, you welcomed the message with the joy given by the Holy Spirit.

ROMANS 8:11, 16, 26–27

If the Spirit of him who raised Jesus from the dead is living in you, he who raised Christ from the dead will also give life to your mortal bodies through his Spirit, who lives in you.... The Spirit himself testifies with our spirit that we are God's children.... The Spirit helps us in our weakness. We do not know what we ought to pray for, but the Spirit himself intercedes for us with groans that words cannot express. And he who searches our hearts knows the mind of the Spirit, because the Spirit intercedes for the saints in accordance with God's will.

ACTS 2:17–18

"'In the last days, God says,
    I will pour out my Spirit on all people.
Your sons and daughters will prophesy,
    your young men will see visions,
    your old men will dream dreams.
Even on my servants, both men and women,
    I will pour out my Spirit in those days,
    and they will prophesy.'"

WORK OF THE HOLY SPIRIT

LUKE 11:10–13

Jesus said to his disciples, "Everyone who asks receives; he who seeks finds; and to him who knocks, the door will be opened."

"Which of you fathers, if your son asks for a fish, will give him a snake instead? Or if he asks for an egg, will give him a scorpion? If you then, though you are evil, know how to give good gifts to your children, how much more will your Father in heaven give the Holy Spirit to those who ask him!"

ACTS 1:4–8

On one occasion, while Jesus was eating with his disciples, he gave them this command: "Do not leave Jerusalem, but wait for the gift my Father promised, which you have heard me speak about. For John baptized with water, but in a few days you will be baptized with the Holy Spirit."

So when they met together, they asked him, "LORD, are you at this time going to restore the kingdom to Israel?"

He said to them: "It is not for you to know the times or dates the Father has set by his own authority. But you will receive power when the Holy Spirit comes on you; and you will be my witnesses in Jerusalem, and in all Judea and Samaria, and to the ends of the earth."

2 CORINTHIANS 3:6, 17–18

God has made us competent as ministers of a new covenant—not of the letter but of the Spirit; for the letter kills, but the Spirit gives life....

Whenever anyone turns to the LORD, the veil is taken away. Now the LORD is the Spirit, and where the Spirit of the LORD is, there is freedom. And we, who with unveiled faces all reflect the LORD's glory, are being transformed into his likeness with ever-increasing glory, which comes from the LORD, who is the Spirit.

1 JOHN 4:1–2

Do not believe every spirit, but test the spirits to see whether they are from God.... This is how you can recognize the Spirit of God: Every spirit that acknowledges that Jesus Christ has come in the flesh is from God.

ACTS 2:38–39

Peter replied "Repent and be baptized, every one of you, in the name of Jesus Christ for the forgiveness of your sins. And you will receive the gift of the Holy Spirit. The promise is for you and your children and for all who are far off—for all whom the LORD our God will call."

WORK OF THE HOLY SPIRIT

EPHESIANS 1:13-14
You also were included in Christ when you heard the
word of truth, the gospel of your salvation. Having
believed, you were marked in him with a seal, the
promised Holy Spirit, who is a deposit guaranteeing
our inheritance until the redemption of those who are
God's possession.

ACTS 2:1-4
When the day of Pentecost was fully come, they were
all with one accord in one place. Suddenly a sound
like the blowing of a violent wind came from heaven,
and filled the whole house where they were sitting.
They saw what seemed to be tongues of fire that sep-
arated and came to rest on each of them. All of them
were filed with the Holy Spirit and began to speak in
other tongues as the Spirit enabled them.

ACTS 15:8

"God, who knows the heart, showed that he accepted them by giving the Holy Spirit to them, just as he did to us," Peter said.

1 CORINTHIANS 6:19-20

Do you not know that your body is a temple of the Holy Sprit, who is in you, whom you have received from God? You are not your own; you were bought with a price.

JOHN 3:5-8

Jesus answered, "I tell you the truth, no one can enter the kingdom of God unless he is born of water and of the Spirit. Flesh gives birth to flesh, but the Spirit gives birth to spirit. You should not be surprised at my saying, 'You must be born again.' The wind blows wherever it pleases. You hear its sound, but you cannot tell where it comes from or where it is going. So it is with everyone born of the Spirit."

WORK OF THE HOLY SPIRIT

JOHN 16:13
"When he, the Spirit of truth comes," Jesus told his disciples, "he will guide you into all truth. He will not speak on his own; he will speak only what he hears, and he will tell you what is yet to come."

MATTHEW 28:19
Jesus said to his disciples, "Therefore go and make disciples of all nations, baptizing them in the name of the Father and of the Son and of the Holy Spirit."

MARK 13:11
Jesus said, "Whenever you are arrested and brought to trial, do not worry beforehand about what to say. Just say whatever is given you at the time, for it is not you speaking, but the Holy Spirit."

THE BODY OF CHRIST (CHURCH)

1 TIMOTHY 3:15
God's household ... is the church of the living God, the pillar and foundation of the truth.

1 CORINTHIANS 12:27-28
You are the body of Christ, and each one of you is a part of it. And in the church God has appointed first of all apostles, second prophets, third teachers, then workers of miracles, also those having gifts of healing, those able to help others, those with gifts of administration, and those speaking in different kinds of tongues.

1 CORINTHIANS 12:12-13
The body is a unit, though it is made up of many parts; and though all its parts are many, they form one body. So it is with Christ. For we were all baptized by one Spirit into one body—whether Jews or Greeks, slave or free—and we were all given the one Spirit to drink.

COLOSSIANS 1:18
Christ is the head of the body, the church; he is the beginning and the firstborn from among the dead, so that in everything he might have the supremacy.

ROMANS 12:4–6
Just as each of us has one body with many members, and these members do not all have the same function, so in Christ we who are many form one body, and each member belongs to all the others. We have different gifts, according to the grace given us. If a man's gift is prophesying, let him use it in proportion to his faith.

HEBREWS 10:25
Let us not give up meeting together, as some are in the habit of doing, but let us encourage one another—and all the more as you see the Day approaching.

HEBREWS 13:17
Obey your leaders and submit to their authority. They keep watch over you as men who must give an account. Obey them so that their work will be a joy, not a burden, for that would be of no advantage to you.

COLOSSIANS 3:16
Let the word of Christ dwell in you richly as you teach and admonish one another with all wisdom, and as you sing psalms, hymns and spiritual songs with gratitude in your hearts to God.

MATTHEW 16:17–18

Jesus replied, "Blessed are you, Simon son of Jonah, for this was not revealed to you by man, but by my Father in heaven. And I tell you that you are Peter, and on this rock I will build my church, and the gates of Hades will not overcome it."

EPHESIANS 2:19–21

You are no longer foreigners and aliens, but fellow citizens with God's people and members of God's household, built on the foundation of the apostles and prophets, with Christ Jesus himself as the chief cornerstone. In him the whole building is joined together and rises to become a holy temple in the LORD.

EPHESIANS 4:11–13

It is God who gave some to be apostles, some to be prophets, some to be evangelists, and some to be pastors and teachers, to prepare God's people for works of service, so that the body of Christ my be built up until we all reach unity in the faith and in the knowledge of the Son of God and become mature, attaining to the whole measure of the fullness of Christ.

THE BODY OF CHRIST (CHURCH)

1 PETER 2:9
You are a chosen people, a royal priesthood, a holy nation, a people belonging to God, that you may declare the praises of him who called you out of darkness into his wonderful light.

EPHESIANS 3:10
God's intent was that now, through the church, the manifold wisdom of God should be made known to the rulers and authorities in the heavenly realms.

HOW DO YOU GROW IN FAITH?

Promises about the Christian Life

Thank you, God, for the great and mighty promises you have made available to me through your love and kindness. As I face the challenges of growing in faith, bring the one I need to my memory so that I may gain strength for my spiritual journey.

ABIDING IN CHRIST

JOHN 15:4–7

Jesus said, "Remain in me, and I will remain in you.
No branch can bear fruit by itself; it must remain in
the vine. Neither can you bear fruit unless you remain
in me.

"I am the vine; you are the branches. If a man
remains in me and I in him, he will bear much fruit;
apart from me you can do nothing. If anyone does
not remain in me, he is like a branch that is thrown
away and withers; such branches are picked up,
thrown into the fire and burned. If you remain in me
and my words remain in you, ask whatever you wish,
and it will be given you."

1 JOHN 2:28

Dear children, continue in him, so that when he
appears we may be confident and unashamed before
him at his coming.

PROVERBS 8:17–19

I love those who love me,
    and those who seek me find me.
With me are riches and honor,
    enduring wealth and prosperity.
My fruit is better than fine gold;
    what I yield surpasses choice silver.

PSALM 119:15–16
I meditate on your precepts
    and consider your ways.
I delight in your decrees;
    I will not neglect your word.

COLOSSIANS 3:16
Let the word of Christ dwell in you richly as you teach
and admonish one another with all wisdom, and as
you sing psalms, hymns and spiritual songs with gratitude in your hearts to God

1 JOHN 2:3–6
We know that we have come to know him if we obey
his commands. The man who says, "I know him," but
does not do what he commands is a liar, and the
truth is not in him. But if anyone obeys his word,
God's love is truly made complete in him. This is how
we know we are in him: Whoever claims to live in him
must walk as Jesus did.

JAMES 4:8, 10
Come near to God and he will come near to you.
Wash your hands, you sinners, and purify your hearts,
you double-minded.... Humble yourselves before the
LORD, and he will lift you up.

ACTS 17:28
In him we live and move and have our being.

PROVERBS 8:34
Blessed is the man who listens to me,
    watching daily at my doors,
    waiting at my doorway.

1 TIMOTHY 4:13
Until I come, devote yourself to the public reading of
Scripture, to preaching and to teaching.

ROMANS 13:14
Clothe yourselves with the LORD Jesus Christ, and do
not think about how to gratify the desires of the
sinful nature.

1 PETER 2:2
Like newborn babies, crave pure spiritual milk, so that
by it you may grow up in your salvation.

ABIDING IN CHRIST

1 JOHN 3:5–6

You know that he appeared so that he might take away our sins. And in him is no sin. No one who lives in him keeps on sinning. No one who continues to sin has either seen him or known him.

2 JOHN 1:9

Anyone who runs ahead and does not continue in the teaching of Christ does not have God; whoever continues in the teaching has both the Father and the Son.

JAMES 1:22

Do not merely listen to the word, and so deceive yourselves. Do what it says.

HEBREWS 2:1–3

We must pay more careful attention, therefore, to what we have heard, so that we do not drift away. For if the message spoken by angels was binding, and every violation and disobedience received its just punishment, how shall we escape if we ignore such a great salvation? This salvation, which was first announced by the LORD, was confirmed to us by those who heard him.

BUILDING YOUR FAITH

HEBREWS 11:1, 3, 6

Faith is being sure of what we hope for and certain of what we do not see....

By faith we understand that the universe was formed at God's command, so that what is seen was not made out of what was visible....

And without faith it is impossible to please God, because anyone who comes to him must believe that he exists and that he rewards those who earnestly seek him.

1 PETER 1:7-9

These have come so that your faith—of greater worth than gold, which perishes even though refined by fire—may be proved genuine and may result in praise, glory and honor when Jesus Christ is revealed. Though you have not seen him, you love him; and even though you do not see him now, you believe in him and are filled with an inexpressible and glorious joy, for you are receiving the goal of your faith, the salvation of your souls.

ROMANS 1:17

In the gospel a righteousness from God is revealed, a righteousness that is by faith from first to last, just as it is written: "The righteous will live by faith."

JOSHUA 1:9
God told Joshua, "Be strong and courageous. Do not be terrified; do not be discouraged, for the LORD your God will be with you wherever you go."

ROMANS 10:17
Faith comes from hearing the message, and the message is heard through the word of Christ.

JAMES 1:5–8
If any of you lacks wisdom, he should ask God, who gives generously to all without finding fault, and it will be given to him. But when he asks, he must believe and not doubt, because he who doubts is like a wave of the sea, blown and tossed by the wind. That man should not think he will receive anything from the LORD; he is a double-minded man, unstable in all he does.

ROMANS 4:20–21
Abraham did not waver through unbelief regarding the promise of God, but was strengthened in his faith and gave glory to God, being fully persuaded that God had power to do what he had promised.

2 CORINTHIANS 4:8–10

We are hard pressed on every side, but not crushed; perplexed, but not in despair; persecuted, but not abandoned; struck down, but not destroyed. We always carry around in our body the death of Jesus, so that the life of Jesus may also be revealed in our body.

ROMANS 8:31

If God is for us, who can be against us?

JUDE 1:20–21

Build yourselves up in your most holy faith and pray in the Holy Spirit. Keep yourselves in God's love as you wait for the mercy of our LORD Jesus Christ to bring you to eternal life.

MARK 9:23

Jesus said, "Everything is possible for him who believes."

JEREMIAH 32:27

The LORD says, "I am the LORD, the God of all mankind. Is anything too hard for me?"

PSALM 73:25–26
Whom have I in heaven but you?
    And earth has nothing I desire besides you.
My flesh and my heart may fail,
    but God is the strength of my heart
    and my portion forever.

JAMES 2:18, 21–24
But someone will say, "You have faith; I have deeds."
Show me your faith without deeds, and I will show
you my faith by what I do.... Was not our ancestor
Abraham considered righteous for what he did when
he offered his son Isaac on the altar? You see that his
faith and his actions were working together, and his
faith was made complete by what he did. And the
scripture was fulfilled that says, "Abraham believed
God, and it was credited to him as righteousness,"
and he was called God's friend. You see that a person
is justified by what he does and not by faith alone.

GALATIANS 5:6
The only thing that counts is faith expressing itself
through love.

EPHESIANS 6:14–16

Stand firm then, with the belt of truth buckled
around your waist, with the breastplate of righteousness in place, and with your feet fitted with the readiness that comes from the gospel of peace. In addition
to all this, take up the shield of faith, with which you
can extinguish all the flaming arrows of the evil one.

JOHN 14:12

"I tell you the truth, anyone who has faith in me will
do what I have been doing. He will do even greater
things than these, because I am going to the Father,"
Jesus told his disciples.

MATTHEW 17:20

Jesus said to his disciples, "If you have faith as small
as a mustard seed, you can say to this mountain,
'Move from here to there' and it will move. Nothing
will be impossible for you."

JAMES 1:3–4

The testing of your faith develops perseverance.
Perseverance must finish its work so that you may be
mature and complete, not lacking anything.

BUILDING YOUR FAITH

2 CORINTHIANS 5:7
We live by faith, not by sight.

LUKE 1:37
"Nothing is impossible with God," the angel told Mary.

1 TIMOTHY 4:9–10
This is a trustworthy saying that deserves full acceptance
(and for this we labor and strive), that we have put
our hope in the living God, who is the Savior of all
men, and especially of those who believe.

PRAISE AND WORSHIP

PSALM 29:2

Ascribe to the LORD the glory due his name;
worship the LORD in the splendor of his
holiness.

EXODUS 15:1–2

I will sing to the LORD,
for he is highly exalted.
The horse and its rider
he has hurled into the sea.
The LORD is my strength and my song;
he has become my salvation.
He is my God, and I will praise him,
my father's God, and I will exalt him.

PSALM 43:4

Then will I go to the altar of God,
to God, my joy and my delight.
I will praise you with the harp,
O God, my God.

1 CHRONICLES 16:25
Great is the LORD and most worthy of praise;
>   he is to be feared above all gods.

PSALM 95:6
Come, let us bow down in worship,
>   let us kneel before the LORD our Maker.

PSALM 100:2
Worship the LORD with gladness;
>   come before him with joyful songs.

HEBREWS 12:28
Since we are receiving a kingdom that cannot be
shaken, let us be thankful, and so worship God
acceptably with reverence and awe.

ROMANS 12:1
I urge you, brothers, in view of God's mercy, to offer
your bodies as living sacrifices, holy and pleasing to
God—this is your spiritual act of worship.

JOHN 4:23-24

Jesus said, "A time is coming and has now come when the true worshipers will worship the Father in spirit and truth, for they are the kind of worshipers the Father seeks. God is spirit, and his worshipers must worship in spirit and in truth."

1 KINGS 8:56-61

Solomon prayed, "Praise be to the LORD, who has given rest to his people Israel just as he promised. Not one word has failed of all the good promises he gave through his servant Moses. May the LORD our God be with us as he was with our fathers; may he never leave us nor forsake us. May he turn our hearts to him, to walk in all his ways and to keep the commands, decrees and regulations he gave our fathers. And may these words of mine, which I have prayed before the LORD, be near to the LORD our God day and night, that he may uphold the cause of his servant and the cause of his people Israel according to each day's need, so that all the peoples of the earth may know that the LORD is God and that there is no other. But your hearts must be fully committed to the LORD our God, to live by his decrees and obey his commands, as at this time."

PRAISE AND WORSHIP

MALACHI 4:2
"For you who revere my name, the sun of righteousness will rise with healing in its wings. And you will go out and leap like calves released from the stall," God said.

PSALM 81:1–3
Sing for joy to God our strength;
    shout aloud to the God of Jacob!
Begin the music, strike the tambourine,
    play the melodious harp and lyre.

Sound the ram's horn at the New Moon,
    and when the moon is full, on the day of our Feast.

PSALM 33:1
Sing joyfully to the LORD, you righteous;
    it is fitting for the upright to praise him.

PSALM 149:5–6
Let the saints rejoice in this honor
    and sing for joy on their beds.

May the praise of God be in their mouths.

Psalm 33:2-3

Praise the Lord with the harp;
>
> make music to him on the ten-stringed lyre.

Sing to him a new song;
>
> play skillfully, and shout for joy.

Revelation 5:13

I heard every creature in heaven and on earth and
under the earth and on the sea, and all that is in
them, singing:

"To him who sits on the throne and to the Lamb
>
> be praise and honor and glory and power,
>
>> for ever and ever!"

Psalm 147:1

How good it is to sing praises to our God,
>
> how pleasant and fitting to praise him!

1 Chronicles 16:9

Sing to the Lord, sing praise to him;
>
> tell of all his wonderful acts.

PRAISE AND WORSHIP

PSALM 149:1–2

Sing to the LORD a new song,
　　his praise in the assembly of the saints.

Let Israel rejoice in their Maker;
　　let the people of Zion be glad in their King.
Let them praise his name with dancing
　　and make music to him with tambourine
　　　　and harp.

PSALM 66:4

All the earth bows down to you, O LORD;
　　they sing praise to you,
　　they sing praise to your name.

JOY OF THE LORD

MATTHEW 25:21

His master replied, "Well done, good and faithful servant! You have been faithful with a few things; I will put you in charge of many things. Come and share your master's happiness!"

JOHN 15:10–12

Jesus said, "If you obey my commands, you will remain in my love, just as I have obeyed my Father's commands and remain in his love. I have told you this so that my joy may be in you and that your joy may be complete. My command is this: Love each other as I have loved you."

PSALM 5:11–12

Let all who take refuge in you be glad;
    let them ever sing for joy.
Spread your protection over them,
    that those who love your name may rejoice in you.
For surely, O LORD, you bless the righteous;
    you surround them with your favor as with a shield.

PROVERBS 17:22
A cheerful heart is good medicine,
    but a crushed spirit dries up the bones

PSALM 45:7-8
You love righteousness and hate wickedness;
    therefore God, your God, has set you above your
    companions
    by anointing you with the oil of joy.
All your robes are fragrant with myrrh and aloes
    and cassia;
    from palaces adorned with ivory
    the music of the strings makes you glad.

PROVERBS 15:13
A happy heart makes the face cheerful,
    but heartache crushes the spirit.

PSALM 118:24
This is the day the LORD has made;
    let us rejoice and be glad in it.

NEHEMIAH 8:10
"Do not grieve, for the joy of the LORD is your
strength," Nehemiah told the people.

PSALM 126:1–3
When the LORD brought back the captives to Zion,
     we were like men who dreamed.
Our mouths were filled with laugher,
     our tongues with songs of joy.
Then it was said among the nations,
     "The LORD has done great things for them."
The LORD has done great things for us,
     and we are filled with joy.

PROVERBS 15:23
A man finds joy in giving an apt reply—
     and how good is a timely word!

ISAIAH 61:10

I delight greatly in the LORD;
    my soul rejoices in my God.
For he has clothed me with garments of salvation
    and arrayed me in a robe of righteousness.

DEUTERONOMY 16:15

The LORD your God will bless you in all your harvest
and in all the work of your hands, and your joy will
be complete.

PSALM 30:11–12

You turned my wailing into dancing;
    you removed my sackcloth and clothed me with joy,
that my heart may sing to you and not be silent.
    O LORD my God, I will give you thanks forever.

PSALM 33:21

In him our hearts rejoice,
    for we trust in his holy name.

PSALM 141:2

May my prayer be set before you like incense;
    may the lifting up of my hands be like the
        evening sacrifice.

PSALM 30:5

    God's favor lasts a lifetime;
weeping may remain for a night,
    but rejoicing comes in the morning.

PSALM 32:11

Rejoice in the LORD and be glad, you righteous;
    sing, all you who are upright in heart!

PSALM 70:4

O Lord, may all who seek you
    rejoice and be glad in you;
May those who love your salvation always say,
    "Let God be exalted!"

JOY OF THE LORD

PSALM 126:5-6
Those who sow in tears
    will reap with songs of joy.
He who goes out weeping,
    carrying seed to sow,
will return with songs of joy,
    carrying sheaves with him.

PSALM 5:11
Let all who take refuge in you be glad, O LORD;
    let them ever sing for joy.
Spread your protection over them,
    that those who love your name may rejoice in you.

LIVING IN LIBERTY

ROMANS 8:1–2
Therefore, there is now no condemnation for those who are in Christ Jesus, because through Christ Jesus the law of the Spirit of life set me free from the law of sin and death.

GALATIANS 5:13
You were called to be free. But do not use your freedom to indulge the sinful nature; rather, serve one another in love.

JAMES 1:25
The man who looks intently into the perfect law that gives freedom, and continues to do this, not forgetting what he has heard, but doing it—he will be blessed in what he does.

JOHN 8:31–32, 36
Jesus said, "If you hold to my teaching, you are really my disciples. Then you will know the truth, and the truth will set you free.... So if the Son sets you free, you will be free indeed."

2 CORINTHIANS 3:17
The LORD is the Spirit, and where the Spirit of the LORD is, there is freedom.

REVELATION 22:16-17
"I, Jesus, have sent my angel to give you this testimony for the churches. I am the Root and the Offspring of David, and the bright Morning Star.
"The Spirit and the bride say, 'Come!' And let him who hears say, 'Come!' Whoever is thirsty, let him come; and whoever wishes, let him take the free gift of the water of life."

GALATIANS 5:1
It is for freedom that Christ has set us free. Stand firm, then, and do not let yourselves be burdened again by a yoke of slavery.

ROMANS 3:22-25
This righteousness from God comes through faith in Jesus Christ to all who believe. There is no difference, for all have sinned and fall short of the glory of God, and are justified freely by his grace through the redemption that came by Christ Jesus. God presented him as a sacrifice of atonement, through faith in his blood.

ISAIAH 52:3
This is what the LORD says:

"You were sold for nothing,
and without money you will be redeemed."

ROMANS 6:22
Now that you have been set free from sin and have
become slaves to God, the benefit you reap leads to
holiness, and the result is eternal life.

GALATIANS 3:13
Christ redeemed us from the curse of the law by
becoming a curse for us, for it is written: "Cursed is
everyone who is hung on a tree."

ROMANS 8:21
Creation itself will be liberated from its bondage to
decay and brought into the glorious freedom of the
children of God.

1 PETER 2:16
Live as free men, but do not use your freedom as a
cover-up for evil; live as servants of God.

GALATIANS 3:14
God redeemed us in order that the blessing given
to Abraham might come to the Gentiles through
Christ Jesus.

ROMANS 7:6
By dying to what once bound us, we have been released
from the law so that we serve in the new way of the
Spirit, and not in the old way of the written code.

SERVING OTHERS

COLOSSIANS 3:23-24

Whatever you do, work at it with all your heart, as working for the LORD, not for men, since you know that you will receive an inheritance from the LORD as a reward. It is the LORD Christ you are serving.

1 PETER 4:10-11

Each one should use whatever gift he has received to serve others, faithfully administering God's grace in its various forms. If anyone speaks, he should do it as one speaking the very words of God. If anyone serves, he should do it with the strength God provides, so that in all things God may be praised through Jesus Christ.

GALATIANS 6:9-10

Let us not become weary in doing good, for at the proper time we will reap a harvest if we do not give up. Therefore, as we have opportunity, let us do good to all people, especially to those who belong to the family of believers.

LUKE 3:11

John answered, "The man with two tunics should share with him who has none, and the one who has food should do the same."

LUKE 10:33-34
Jesus told a parable. "A Samaritan, as he traveled, came where the man was; and when he saw him, he took pity on him. He went to him and bandaged his wounds, pouring on oil and wine. Then he put the man on his own donkey, took him to an inn and took care of him. The next day he took out two silver coins and gave them to the innkeeper. 'Look after him,' he said, 'and when I return, I will reimburse you for any extra expense you may have.'"

1 CORINTHIANS 12:5
There are different kinds of service, but the same LORD.

1 TIMOTHY 3:13
Those who have served well gain an excellent standing and great assurance in their faith in Christ Jesus.

PHILIPPIANS 2:3-4
Do nothing out of selfish ambition or vain conceit, but in humility consider others better than yourselves. Each of you should look not only to your own interests, but also to the interests of others.

EPHESIANS 6:7–8
Serve wholeheartedly, as if you were serving the LORD, not men, because you know that the LORD will reward everyone for whatever good he does.

1 PETER 5:2
Be shepherds of God's flock that is under your care, serving as overseers—not because you must, but because you are willing, as God wants you to be; not greedy for money, but eager to serve.

ROMANS 12:11–13
Never be lacking in zeal, but keep your spiritual fervor, serving the LORD. Be joyful in hope, patient in affliction, faithful in prayer. Share with God's people who are in need. Practice hospitality.

MARK 9:35
Jesus said to his disciples, "If anyone wants to be first, he must be the very last, and the servant of all."

SERVING OTHERS

DEUTERONOMY 15:11
There will always be poor people in the land. Therefore
I command you to be openhanded toward your brothers
and toward the poor and needy in your land.

HEBREWS 13:16
Do not forget to do good and to share with others,
for with such sacrifices God is pleased.

SERVING GOD

DEUTERONOMY 13:4
It is the LORD your God you must follow, and him you must revere. Keep his commands and obey him; serve him and hold fast to him.

JOSHUA 24:15
"If serving the LORD seems undesirable to you, then choose for yourselves this day whom you will serve.... But as for me and my household, we will serve the LORD," Joshua said to the tribes of Israel.

1 SAMUEL 12:24
"Be sure to fear the LORD and serve him faithfully with all your heart; consider what great things he has done for you," Samuel said.

1 CHRONICLES 28:9
David told Solomon, "Acknowledge the God of your father, and serve him with wholehearted devotion and with a willing mind, for the LORD searches every heart and understands every motive behind the thoughts."

PSALM 2:10–11
Therefore, you kings, be wise;
    be warned, you rulers of the earth.
Serve the LORD with fear
    and rejoice with trembling.

JOB 36:11
If they obey and serve him,
    they will spend the rest of their days in prosperity
    and their years in contentment.

JEREMIAH 15:19
This is what the LORD says:

"If you repent, I will restore you
    that you may serve me;
if you utter worthy, not worthless, words,
    you will be my spokesman."

DEUTERONOMY 10:12
What does the LORD your God ask of you but to fear the LORD your God, to walk in all his ways, to love him, to serve the LORD your God with all your heart and with all your soul.

MATTHEW 4:10
Jesus said, "Worship the LORD your God, and serve him only."

MATTHEW 6:24
Jesus said, "No one can serve two masters. Either he will hate the one and love the other, or he will be devoted to the one and despise the other. You cannot serve both God and Money."

Isaiah 56:6–7

Foreigners who bind themselves to the Lord
    to serve him,
to love the name of the Lord,
    and to worship him,
all who keep the Sabbath without desecrating it
    and who hold fast to my covenant—
these will I bring to my holy mountain
    and give them joy in my house of prayer.

BEING A WITNESS

MATTHEW 5:14–16

Jesus said, "You are the light of the world. A city on a hill cannot be hidden. Neither do people light a lamp and put it under a bowl. Instead they put it on its stand, and it gives light to everyone in the house. In the same way, let your light shine before men, that they may see your good deeds and praise your Father in heaven."

1 PETER 3:15–16

In your hearts set apart Christ as LORD. Always be prepared to give an answer to everyone who asks you to give the reason for the hope that you have. But do this with gentleness and respect, keeping a clear conscience, so that those who speak maliciously against your good behavior in Christ may be ashamed of
their slander.

LUKE 12:8

Jesus said, "I tell you, whoever acknowledges me before men, the Son of Man will also acknowledge him before the angels of God."

JOHN 13:35
Jesus said, "By this all men will know that you are my disciples, if you love one another."

ISAIAH 43:10
"You are my witnesses," declares the LORD,
    "and my servant whom I have chosen,
so that you may know and believe me
    and understand that I am he.
Before me no god was formed,
    nor will there be one after me,
I, even I, am the LORD.
    and apart from me there is no savior."

1 JOHN 4:15
If anyone acknowledges that Jesus is the Son of God, God live in him and he in God.

DANIEL 12:3
Those who are wise will shine like the brightness of the heavens, and those who lead many to righteousness, like the stars for ever and ever.

PSALM 96:2–3
Sing to the LORD, praise his name;
   proclaim his salvation day after day.
Declare his glory among the nations,
   his marvelous deeds among all peoples.

PHILIPPIANS 2:10–11
At the name of Jesus every knee should bow,
   in heaven and on earth and under the earth
and every tongue confess that Jesus Christ is LORD,
   to the glory of God the Father.

JAMES 5:19–20
If one of you should wander from the truth and someone should bring him back, remember this: Whoever
turns a sinner from the error of his way will save him
from death and cover over a multitude of sins.

BEING A WITNESS

ACTS 1:8
Jesus said to them, "You will be my witnesses in Jerusalem, and in all Judea and Samaria, and to the ends of the earth."

MARK 16:15
Jesus said to them, "Go into all the world and preach the good news to all creation."

MATTHEW 24:14
"This gospel of the kingdom will be preached in the whole world as a testimony to all nations, and then the end will come," Jesus said to his disciples.

CLAIMING GOD'S PROMISES

DEUTERONOMY 11:22–24
If you carefully observe all these commands I am giving you to follow—to love the LORD your God, to walk in all his ways and to hold fast to him—then the LORD will drive out all these nations before you, and you will dispossess nations larger and stronger than you. Every place where you set your foot will be yours.

MARK 11:23–24
Jesus said, "I tell you the truth, if anyone says to this mountain, 'Go, throw yourself into the sea,' and does not doubt in his heart but believes that what he says will happen, it will be done for him. Therefore I tell you, whatever you ask for in prayer, believe that you have received it, and it will be yours."

HEBREWS 10:35–37
Do not throw away your confidence; it will be richly rewarded. You need to persevere so that when you have done the will of God, you will receive what he has promised. For in just a very little while,

"He who is coming will come and will not delay."

DEUTERONOMY 11:26-28

I am setting before you today a blessing and a curse—
the blessing if you obey the commands of the LORD
your God that I am giving you today; the curse if you
disobey the commands of the LORD your God and turn
from the way that I command you today by following
other gods, which you have not known.

2 PETER 1:3-8

God's divine power has given us everything we need
for life and godliness through our knowledge of him
who called us by his own glory and goodness.
Through these he has given us his very great and
precious promises, so that through them you may par-
ticipate in the divine nature and escape the corruption
in the world caused by evil desires.
For this very reason, make every effort to add to your
faith goodness; and to goodness, knowledge; and to
knowledge, self-control; and to self-control, perseverance; and to perseverance, godliness; and to godliness,
brotherly kindness; and to brotherly kindness, love.
For if you possess these qualities in increasing measure,
they will keep you from being ineffective and unpro-
ductive in your knowledge of our LORD Jesus Christ.

HEBREWS 11:1, 6
Faith is being sure of what we hope for and certain of what we do not see.... And without faith it is impossible to please God, because anyone who comes to him must believe that he exists and that he rewards those who earnestly seek him.

ISAIAH 1:19–20
"If you are willing and obedient,
    you will eat the best from the land;
but if you resist and rebel,
    you will be devoured by the sword."
        For the mouth of the LORD has spoken.

GALATIANS 3:26–29
You are all sons of God through faith in Christ Jesus, for all of you who were baptized into Christ have clothed yourselves with Christ. There is neither Jew nor Greek, slave nor free, male nor female, for you are all one in Christ Jesus. If you belong to Christ, then you are Abraham's seed, and heirs according to the promise.

CLAIMING GOD'S PROMISES

2 CORINTHIANS 1:20–22
No matter how many promises God has made, they
are "Yes" in Christ. And so through him the "Amen" is
spoken by us to the glory of God. Now it is God who
makes both us and you stand firm in Christ. He
anointed us, set his seal of ownership on us, and put
his Spirit in our hearts as a deposit, guaranteeing
what is to come.

HEBREWS 10:22–23
Let us draw near to God with a sincere heart in full
assurance of faith, having our hearts sprinkled to cleanse
us from a guilty conscience and having our bodies
washed with pure water. Let us hold unswervingly to the
hope we profess, for he who promised is faithful.

PSALM 145:13–16
The LORD is faithful to all his promises
    and loving toward all he has made.
The LORD upholds all those who fall
    and lifts up all who are bowed down.
The eyes of all look to you,
    and you give them their food at the proper time.
You open your hand
    and satisfy the desires of every living thing.

MATTHEW 6:33

Jesus said, "Seek first his kingdom and his righteousness, and all these things will be given to you as well."

JOSHUA 23:14

"You know with all your heart and soul that not one of all the good promises the LORD your God gave you has failed. Every promise has been fulfilled; not one has failed," Joshua said.

1 KINGS 8:56–58

"Praise be to the LORD, who has given rest to his people Israel just as he promised. Not one word has failed of all the good promises he gave through his servant Moses. May the LORD our God be with us as he was with our fathers; may he never leave us nor forsake us. May he turn our hearts to him, to walk in all his ways and to keep the commands, decrees and regulations he gave our fathers," Soloman said.

HEBREWS 6:12
We do not want you to become lazy, but to imitate those who through faith and patience inherit what has been promised.

PSALM 119:50
My comfort in my suffering is this:
   Your promise preserves my life.

JOSHUA 1:7
God said, "Be strong and very courageous. Be careful to obey all the law my servant Moses gave you; do not turn from it to the right or to the left, that you may be successful wherever you go."

CHAPTER

7

WHAT DOES GOD GIVE TO HIS CHILDREN?

Promises about God's Perfect Gifts for You

Thank you, God, that you have adopted me as your very own child. You know my every need and desire, and you give me perfect gifts. Thank you, my good Father, that you want more for me than even I want for myself.

AMAZING GRACE

EPHESIANS 2:8-10
It is by grace you have been saved, through faith—and this not from yourselves, it is the gift of God—not by works, so that no one can boast. For we are God's workmanship, created in Christ Jesus to do good works, which God prepared in advance for us to do.

PSALM 116:5
The LORD is gracious and righteous;
    our God is full of compassion.

EPHESIANS 2:6-7
God raised us up with Christ and seated us with him in the heavenly realms in Christ Jesus, in order that in the coming ages he might show the incomparable riches of his grace, expressed in his kindness to us in Christ Jesus.

ROMANS 5:1-2
Since we have been justified through faith, we have peace with God through our LORD Jesus Christ, through whom we have gained access by faith into this grace in which we now stand. And we rejoice in the hope of the glory of God.

ROMANS 5:17

If, by the trespass of the one man, death reigned through that one man, how much more will those who receive God's abundant provision of grace and of the gift of righteousness reign in life through the one man, Jesus Christ.

2 CORINTHIANS 8:9

You know the grace of our LORD Jesus Christ, that though he was rich, yet for your sakes he became poor, so that you through his poverty might become rich.

JOHN 1:16

From the fullness of God's grace we have all received one blessing after another.

2 CORINTHIANS 9:8

God is able to make all grace abound to you, so that in all things at all times, having all that you need, you will abound in every good work.

2 CORINTHIANS 12:9

The LORD said to me, "My grace is sufficient for you, for my power is made perfect in weakness." Therefore I will boast all the more gladly about my weaknesses, so that Christ's power may rest on me.

1 PETER 5:10

The God of all grace, who called you to his eternal glory in Christ, after you have suffered a little while, will himself restore you and make you strong, firm and steadfast.

2 PETER 1:2

Grace and peace be yours in abundance through the knowledge of God and of Jesus our LORD.

PSALM 145:8

The LORD is gracious and compassionate,
    slow to anger and rich in love.

EPHESIANS 1:5–7

God predestined us to be adopted as his sons through Jesus Christ, in accordance with his pleasure and will— to the praise of his glorious grace, which he has freely given us in the One he loves. In him we have redemption through his blood, the forgiveness of sins, in accordance with the riches of God's grace.

JAMES 4:6

God gives us more grace.

AMAZING GRACE

HEBREWS 4:16

Let us ... approach the throne of grace with confidence, so that we may receive mercy and find grace to help us in our time of need.

LAMENTATIONS 3:22

Because of the LORD's great love we are not consumed,

for his compassions never fail.

A SENSE OF BELONGING

1 SAMUEL 12:22
For the sake of his great name the LORD will not reject
his people, because the LORD was pleased to make you
his own.

ISAIAH 49:15–16
"Can a mother forget the baby at her breast
    and have no compassion on the child
        she has borne?
Though she may forget,
    I will not forget you!
See, I have engraved you on the palms of my hands;
    your walls are ever before me,"
        declares the LORD.

1 PETER 2:9
You are a chosen people, a royal priesthood, a holy
nation, a people belonging to God, that you may
declare the praises of him who called you out of darkness into his wonderful light.

EPHESIANS 1:13

You also were included in Christ when you heard the word of truth, the gospel of your salvation. Having believed, you were marked in him with a seal, the promised Holy Spirit.

PSALM 95:6–7

Come, let us bow down in worship,
    let us kneel before the LORD our Maker;
for he is our God
    and we are the people of his pasture,
    the flock under his care.

EPHESIANS 2:10

We are God's workmanship, created in Christ Jesus to do good works, which God prepared in advance for us to do.

COLOSSIANS 3:12

As God's chosen people, holy and dearly loved, clothe yourselves with compassion, kindness, humility, gentleness and patience.

PHILIPPIANS 3:20
Our citizenship is in heaven. And we eagerly await a
Savior from there, the LORD Jesus Christ.

MATTHEW 10:29–31
"Are not two sparrows sold for a penny? Yet not one
of them will fall to the ground apart from the will of
your Father. And even the very hairs of your head are
all numbered. So don't be afraid; you are worth more
than many sparrows," Jesus said.

PSALM 139:13–14
O LORD, you created my inmost being;
    you knit me together in my mother's womb.
I praise you because I am fearfully and wonderfully
made;
    your works are wonderful,
    I know that full well.

ISAIAH 43:1
This is what the LORD says—
>he who created you, O Jacob,
>he who formed you, O Israel:
"Fear not, for I have redeemed you;
>I have summoned you by name; you are mine."

JEREMIAH 31:3
The LORD appeared to us in the past, saying:

"I have loved you with an everlasting love;
>I have drawn you with loving-kindness."

PSALM 100:3
Know that the LORD is God.
>It is he who made us, and we are his;
>we are his people, the sheep of his pasture.

1 CORINTHIANS 12:27
You are the body of Christ, and each one of you is a part of it.

EPHESIANS 1:5-6
God predestined us to be adopted as his sons through Jesus Christ, in accordance with his pleasure and will—to the praise of his glorious grace, which he has freely given us in the One he loves.

DEUTERONOMY 7:6
You are a people holy to the LORD your God. The LORD your God has chosen you out of all the peoples on the face of the earth to be his people, his treasured possession.

A SENSE OF BELONGING

COLOSSIANS 2:9–10
In Christ all the fullness of the Deity lives in bodily form, and you have been given fullness in Christ, who is the head over every power and authority.

1 THESSALONIANS 5:5, 8–10
You are all sons of the light and sons of the day. We do not belong to the night or to the darkness.... But since we belong to the day, let us be self-controlled, putting on faith and love as a breastplate, and the hope of salvation as a helmet. For God did not appoint us to suffer wrath but to receive salvation through our LORD Jesus Christ. He died for us so that, whether we are awake or asleep, we may live together with him.

ENCOURAGEMENT

2 THESSALONIANS 2:16–17
May our LORD Jesus Christ himself and God our
Father, who loved us and by his grace gave us eternal
encouragement and good hope, encourage your hearts
and strengthen you in every good deed and word.

1 THESSALONIANS 5:11
Encourage one another and build each other up, just
as in fact you are doing.

ZEPHANIAH 3:17
The LORD your God is with you,
    he is mighty to save.
He will take great delight in you,
    he will quiet you with his love,
    he will rejoice over you with singing.

JOHN 14:16
Jesus said, "I will ask the Father, and he will give you
another Counselor to be with you forever."

PSALM 10:17
You hear, O LORD, the desire of the afflicted;
    you encourage them, and you listen to their cry.

LAMENTATIONS 3:25–26
The LORD is good to those whose hope is in him,
    to the one who seeks him;
it is good to wait quietly
    for the salvation of the LORD.

JEREMIAH 29:11
"I know the plans I have for you," declares the LORD,
"plans to prosper you and not to harm you, plans to
give you hope and a future."

PSALM 55:22
Cast your cares on the LORD
    and he will sustain you;
    he will never let the righteous fall.

LAMENTATIONS 3:22–23
Because of the LORD's great love we are not consumed,
    for his compassions never fail.
They are new every morning;
    great is your faithfulness.

PSALM 68:19
Praise be to the Lord, to God our Savior,
    who daily bears our burdens.

GALATIANS 6:9
Let us not become weary in doing good, for at the
proper time we will reap a harvest if we do not give up.

HEBREWS 6:10
God is not unjust; he will not forget your work and
the love you have shown him as you have helped his
people and continue to help them.

ENCOURAGEMENT

ROMANS 15:4–5

Everything that was written in the past was written to teach us, so that through endurance and the encouragement of the Scriptures we might have hope. May the God who gives endurance and encouragement give you a spirit of unity among yourselves as you follow Christ Jesus.

PSALM 23:1–4

The LORD is my shepherd, I shall not be in want.

He makes me lie down in green pastures,
he leads me beside quiet waters,

he restores my soul.
He guides me in paths of righteousness

for his name's sake.
Even though I walk

through the valley of the shadow of death,
I will fear no evil,

for you are with me;
your rod and your staff,

they comfort me.

MATTHEW 11:28–29

Jesus said, "Come to me, all you who are weary and burdened, and I will give you rest. Take my yoke upon you and learn from me, for I am gentle and humble in heart, and you will find rest for your souls."

DEUTERONOMY 31:6

Moses said, "Be strong and courageous. Do not be afraid or terrified ... for the LORD your God goes with you; he will never leave you nor forsake you."

ISAIAH 41:13

"I am the LORD, your God,
    who takes hold of your right hand
and says to you, Do not fear;
    I will help you."

PSALM 145:14

The LORD upholds all those who fall
    and lifts up all who are bowed down.

PHILIPPIANS 1:6
God who began a good work in you will carry it on to completion until the day of Christ Jesus.

JOHN 14:1-3
Jesus said, "Do not let your hearts be troubled. Trust in God; trust also in me. In my Father's house are many rooms; if it were not so, I would have told you. I am going there to prepare a place for you. And if I go and prepare a place for you, I will come back and take you to be with me that you also may be where I am."

PSALM 31:24
Be strong and take heart,
    all you who hope in the LORD.

CONTENTMENT

PHILIPPIANS 4:11–12
I have learned to be content whatever the circumstances. I know what it is to be in need, and I know what it is to have plenty. I have learned the secret of being content in any and every situation, whether well fed or hungry, whether living in plenty or in want.

PROVERBS 19:23
The fear of the LORD leads to life:
    Then one rests content, untouched by trouble.

1 TIMOTHY 6:6–7
Godliness with contentment is great gain. For we brought nothing into the world, and we can take nothing out of it.

PSALM 16:2
I said to the LORD, "You are my Lord;
    apart from you I have no good thing."

ECCLESIASTES 2:24
A man can do nothing better than to eat and drink and find satisfaction in his work. This too, I see, is from the hand of God.

PSALM 103:5
The LORD satisfies your desires with good things
  so that your youth is renewed like the eagle's.

PSALM 37:4
Delight yourself in the LORD
  and he will give you the desires of your heart.

LUKE 6:21
Jesus said, "Blessed are you who hunger now,
  for you will be satisfied.
Blessed are you who weep now,
  for you will laugh."

PSALM 107:8-9
Let them give thanks to the LORD
  for his unfailing love
  and his wonderful deeds for men,
for he satisfies the thirsty
  and fills the hungry with good things.

PSALM 90:14
Satisfy us in the morning with your unfailing love,
> O LORD,
>> that we may sing for joy and be glad all our days.

PSALM 91:16
"With long life will I satisfy him
> and show him my salvation,"
> says the LORD.

PROVERBS 15:15
The cheerful heart has a continual feast.

PSALM 46:10
"Be still, and know that I am God;
> I will be exalted among the nations,
> I will be exalted in the earth."

CONTENTMENT

PSALM 107:28-30

They cried out to the LORD in their trouble,
> and he brought them out of their distress.
He stilled the storm to a whisper;
> the waves of the sea were hushed.
They were glad when it grew calm,
> and he guided them to their desired haven.

PSALM 4:8

I will lie down and sleep in peace,
> for you alone, O LORD,
> make me dwell in safety.

PSALM 23:1-2

The LORD is my shepherd, I shall not be in want.
> He makes me lie down in green pastures,
he leads me beside quiet waters.

PROVERBS 1:33

Whoever listens to wisdom will live in safety
    and be at ease, without fear of harm.

2 PETER 1:3

God's divine power has given us everything we need
for life and godliness through our knowledge of him
who called us by his own glory and goodness.

2 CORINTHIANS 9:8–11

    God is able to make all grace abound to you, so
that in all things at all times, having all that you
need, you
    will abound in every good work. As it is written:
"He has scattered abroad his gifts to the poor;
    his righteousness endures forever."
Now he who supplies seed to the sower and bread for
food will also supply and increase your store of seed
and will enlarge the harvest of your righteousness.
You will be made rich in every way so that you can be
generous on every occasion, and through us your generosity will result in thanksgiving to God.

CONTENTMENT

PSALM 37:16–17
Better the little that the righteous have
    than the wealth of many wicked;
For the power of the wicked will be broken,
    But the LORD upholds the righteous.

JEREMIAH 31:25
"I will refresh the weary and satisfy the faint," says
the LORD.

PHILIPPIANS 4:19
My God will meet all your needs according to his glorious riches in Christ Jesus.

THE FREEDOM OF FORGIVENESS

GALATIANS 5:1
It is for freedom that Christ has set us free.

PSALM 119:45
I will walk about in freedom,
    for I have sought out your precepts, O LORD.

ACTS 2:38
"Repent and be baptized, every one of you, in the
name of Jesus Christ for the forgiveness of your sins.
And you will receive the gift of the Holy Spirit,"
said Peter.

ACTS 10:43
"All the prophets testify about Jesus that everyone
who believes in him receives forgiveness of sins
through his name," Peter said.

GALATIANS 5:13
You ... were called to be free.

EPHESIANS 1:3–7
Praise be to the God and Father of our Lord Jesus
Christ, who has blessed us in the heavenly realms with
every spiritual blessing in Christ. For he chose us in
him before the creation of the world to be holy and
blameless in his sight. In love he predestined us to be
adopted as his sons through Jesus Christ, in accordance with his pleasure and will—to the praise of his
glorious grace, which he has freely given us in the
One he loves. In Christ we have redemption through
his blood, the forgiveness of sins, in accordance with
the riches of God's grace.

JAMES 1:25
The man who looks intently into the perfect law that
gives freedom, and continues to do this, not forgetting
what he has heard, but doing it—he will be blessed in
what he does.

HEBREWS 9:15
Christ is the mediator of a new covenant, that those
who are called may receive the promised eternal inheritance—now that he has died as a ransom to set them
free from the sins committed under the first covenant.

ROMANS 8:21
Creation itself will be liberated from its bondage to decay and brought into the glorious freedom of the children of God.

COLOSSIANS 1:22-23
God has reconciled you by Christ's physical body through death to present you holy in his sight, without blemish and free from accusation—if you continue in your faith, established and firm, not moved from the hope held out in the gospel.

JOHN 8:36
"If the Son sets you free, you will be free indeed," Jesus said.

ROMANS 8:1-2
There is now no condemnation for those who are in Christ Jesus, because through Christ Jesus the law of the Spirit of life set me free from the law of sin and death.

EPHESIANS 3:12
In Christ and through faith in him we may approach God with freedom and confidence.

COLOSSIANS 2:13-14
When you were dead in your sins and in the uncircumcision of your sinful nature, God made you alive with Christ. He forgave us all our sins, having canceled the written code, with its regulations, that was against us and that stood opposed to us; he took it away, nailing it to the cross.

CERTAINTY IN GOD

ROMANS 8:38–39
Neither death nor life, neither angels nor demons,
neither the present nor the future, nor any powers,
neither height nor depth, nor anything else in all
creation, will be able to separate us from the love of
God that is in Christ Jesus our LORD.

ISAIAH 54:10
"Though the mountains be shaken
    and the hills be removed,
yet my unfailing love for you will not be shaken
    or my covenant of peace be removed,"
    says the LORD, who has compassion on you.

JOHN 10:27–29
Jesus said, "My sheep listen to my voice; I know
them, and they follow me. I give them eternal life,
and they shall never perish; no one can snatch them
out of my hand. My Father, who has given them to
me, is greater than all; no one can snatch them out of
my Father's hand."

2 TIMOTHY 1:12

I know whom I have believed, and am convinced that he is able to guard what I have entrusted to him for that day.

1 TIMOTHY 3:13

Those who have served well gain an excellent standing and great assurance in their faith in Christ Jesus.

HEBREWS 10:19, 22

Since we have confidence to enter the Most Holy Place by the blood of Jesus ... let us draw near to God with a sincere heart in full assurance of faith, having our hearts sprinkled to cleanse us from a guilty conscience and having our bodies washed with pure water.

1 JOHN 5:14–15

This is the confidence we have in approaching God: that if we ask anything according to his will, he hears us. And if we know that he hears us—whatever we ask—we know that we have what we asked of him.

HEBREWS 13:6
We say with confidence,

"The LORD is my helper; I will not be afraid.
 What can man do to me?"

PSALM 27:3, 5
Though an army besiege me,
 my heart will not fear;
though war break out against me,
 even then will I be confident....
For in the day of trouble
 God will keep me safe in his dwelling.

PSALM 23:4
Even though I walk
 through the valley of the shadow of death,
I will fear no evil,
 for you are with me, O LORD;
your rod and your staff,
 they comfort me.

CERTAINTY IN GOD

ISAIAH 32:17
The fruit of righteousness will be peace;
    the effect of righteousness will be quietness
        and confidence forever.

PROVERBS 3:26
The LORD will be your confidence
    and will keep your foot from being snared.

HEBREWS 4:16
Let us then approach the throne of grace with confidence, so that we may receive mercy and find grace to help us in our time of need.

1 JOHN 4:16-17
We know and rely on the love God has for us. God is love. Whoever lives in love lives in God, and God in him. In this way, love is made complete among us so that we will have confidence on the day of judgment, because in this world we are like him.

1 JOHN 3:21-24

Dear friends, if our hearts do not condemn us, we have confidence before God and receive from him anything we ask, because we obey his commands and do what pleases him. And this is his command: to believe in the name of his Son, Jesus Christ, and to love one another as he commanded us. Those who obey his commands live in him, and he in them. And this is how we know that he lives in us: We know it by the Spirit he gave us.

JEREMIAH 17:5,7-8

This is what the LORD says:

"Blessed is the man who trusts in the LORD,
　　whose confidence is in him.
He will be like a tree planted by the water
　　that sends out its roots by the stream.
It does not fear when heat comes;
　　its leaves are always green.
It has no worries in a year of drought
　　and never fails to bear fruit."

CERTAINITY IN GOD

HEBREWS 10:35–37
Do not throw away your confidence; it will be richly
rewarded. You need to persevere so that when you
have done the will of God, you will receive what he
has promised. For in just a very little while,

"He who is coming will come and will not delay."

HEBREWS 11:1
Faith is being sure of what we hope for and certain of
what we do not see.

1 JOHN 2:28
Continue in Christ, so that when he appears we may be
confident and unashamed before him at his coming.

STRENGTH TO RESIST TEMPTATION

1 CORINTHIANS 10:13
No temptation has seized you except what is common to man. And God is faithful; he will not let you be tempted beyond what you can bear. But when you are tempted, he will also provide a way out so that you can stand up under it.

JAMES 1:12
Blessed is the man who perseveres under trial, because when he has stood the test, he will receive the crown of life that God has promised to those who love him.

JAMES 4:7
Submit yourselves ... to God. Resist the devil, and he will flee from you.

HEBREWS 2:18
Because Jesus himself suffered when he was tempted, he is able to help those who are being tempted.

GALATIANS 5:1
It is for freedom that Christ has set us free. Stand firm, then, and do not let yourselves be burdened again by a yoke of slavery.

HEBREWS 4:14-16
Since we have a great high priest who has gone through the heavens, Jesus the Son of God, let us hold firmly to the faith we profess. For we do not have a high priest who is unable to sympathize with our weaknesses, but we have one who has been tempted in every way, just as we are—yet was without sin. Let us then approach the throne of grace with confidence, so that we may receive mercy and find grace to help us in our time of need.

EPHESIANS 6:10-11
Be strong in the LORD and in his mighty power. Put on the full armor of God so that you can take your stand against the devil's schemes.

PSALM 119:11
I have hidden your word in my heart, O LORD,
    that I might not sin against you.

ROMANS 6:14
Sin shall not be your master, because you are not under law, but under grace.

2 CORINTHIANS 12:9

The LORD said to me, "My grace is sufficient for you, for my power is made perfect in weakness." Therefore I will boast all the more gladly about my weaknesses, so that Christ's power may rest on me.

1 PETER 1:7

Trials have come so that your faith—of greater worth than gold, which perishes even though refined by fire—may be proved genuine and may result in praise, glory and honor when Jesus Christ is revealed.

PSALM 46:1-3

God is our refuge and strength,
    an ever-present help in trouble.
Therefore we will not fear, though the earth give way
    and the mountains fall into the heart of the sea,
though its waters roar and foam
    and the mountains quake with their surging.

STRENGTH TO RESIST TEMPTATION

PSALM 68:19
Praise be to the Lord, to God our Savior,
    who daily bears our burdens.

PROVERBS 28:13
He who conceals his sins does not prosper,
    but whoever confesses and renounces them
        finds mercy.

ISAIAH 59:1
Surely the arm of the LORD is not too short to save,
    nor his ear too dull to hear.

JOSHUA 1:9
"Be strong and courageous. Do not be terrified; do
not be discouraged, for the LORD your God will be
with you wherever you go," the Lord told Joshua.

1 JOHN 4:4
The one who is in you is greater than the one who is
in the world.

1 JOHN 1:9

If we confess our sins, God is faithful and just and will forgive us our sins and purify us from all unrighteousness.

JUDE 1:24–25

To him who is able to keep you from falling and to present you before his glorious presence without fault and with great joy—to the only God our Savior be glory, majesty, power and authority, through Jesus Christ our LORD, before all ages, now and forevermore! Amen.

2 PETER 2:9

The LORD knows how to rescue godly men from trials.

2 TIMOTHY 4:17

The LORD stood at my side and gave me strength.

PHILIPPIANS 4:13
I can do everything through Christ who gives me strength.

HABAKKUK 3:19
The Sovereign LORD is my strength;
 he makes my feet like the feet of a deer,
 he enables me to go on the heights.

PATIENCE TO ENDURE HARD TIMES

JAMES 1:2-4, 12

Consider it pure joy, my brothers, whenever you face trials of many kinds, because you know that the testing of your faith develops perseverance. Perseverance must finish its work so that you may be mature and complete, not lacking anything.... Blessed is the man who perseveres under trial, because when he has stood the test, he will receive the crown of life that God has promised to those who love him.

ROMANS 8:38-39

Neither death nor life, neither angels nor demons, neither the present nor the future, nor any powers, neither height nor depth, nor anything else in all creation, will be able to separate us from the love of God that is in Christ Jesus our LORD.

PSALM 121:1-2

I lift up my eyes to the hills—
    where does my help come from?
My help comes from the LORD,
    the Maker of heaven and earth.

2 CORINTHIANS 4:8–10, 16–18

We are hard pressed on every side, but not crushed;
perplexed, but not in despair; persecuted, but not
abandoned; struck down, but not destroyed. We
always carry around in our body the death of Jesus,
so that the life of Jesus may also be revealed in our
body.... Therefore we do not lose heart. Though outwardly we are wasting away, yet inwardly we are
being renewed day by day. For our light and momentary troubles are achieving for us an eternal glory that
far outweighs them all. So we fix our eyes not on
what is seen, but on what is unseen. For what is seen
is temporary, but what is unseen is eternal.

PSALM 147:3

The LORD heals the brokenhearted
    and binds up their wounds.

ISAIAH 41:10

"Do not fear, for I am with you;
    do not be dismayed, for I am your God.
I will strengthen you and help you;
    I will uphold you with my righteous right hand,"
        says the LORD.

ROMANS 8:28
In all things God works for the good of those who love him, who have been called according to his purpose.

ISAIAH 43:2
"When you pass through the waters,
    I will be with you;
and when you pass through the rivers,
    they will not sweep over you.
When you walk through the fire,
    you will not be burned;
    the flames will not set you ablaze,"
        says the LORD.

PHILIPPIANS 4:6–7
Do not be anxious about anything, but in everything, by prayer and petition, with thanksgiving, present your requests to God. And the peace of God, which transcends all understanding, will guard your hearts and your minds in Christ Jesus.

PATIENCE TO ENDURE HARD TIMES

PSALM 31:7
I will be glad and rejoice in your love, O LORD,
for you saw my affliction
and knew the anguish of my soul.

PSALM 138:7
Though I walk in the midst of trouble,
you preserve my life, O LORD;
you stretch out your hand against the anger of my foes,
with your right hand you save me.

ISAIAH 40:31
Those who hope in the LORD
will renew their strength.
They will soar on wings like eagles;
they will run and not grow weary,
they will walk and not be faint.

Lamentations 3:24–26

I say to myself, "The Lord is my portion;
therefore I will wait for him."

The Lord is good to those whose hope is in him,
to the one who seeks him;
it is good to wait quietly
for the salvation of the Lord.

Nahum 1:7

The Lord is good,
a refuge in times of trouble.
He cares for those who trust in him.

Matthew 6:34

Jesus said to his disciples, "Do not worry about
tomorrow, for tomorrow will worry about itself."

John 14:1

Jesus said, "Do not let your hearts be troubled. Trust
in God; trust also in me."

PATIENCE TO ENDURE HARD TIMES

2 CORINTHIANS 1:3-4

Praise be to the God and Father of our LORD Jesus Christ, the Father of compassion and the God of all comfort, who comforts us in all our troubles, so that we can comfort those in any trouble with the comfort we ourselves have received from God.

HEBREWS 12:10-11

Our fathers disciplined us for a little while as they thought best; but God disciplines us for our good, that we may share in his holiness. No discipline seems pleasant at the time, but painful. Later on, however, it produces a harvest of righteousness and peace for those who have been trained by it.

HEBREWS 13:5

God has said,
    "Never will I leave you;
    never will I forsake you."

EXODUS 14:14

"The LORD will fight for you; you need only to be still," Moses said.

1 PETER 5:7
Cast all your anxiety on God because he cares for you.

PHILIPPIANS 4:13
I can do everything through God who gives me strength.

1 PETER 5:10
The God of all grace, who called you to his eternal glory in Christ, after you have suffered a little while, will himself restore you and make you strong, firm and steadfast. To him be the power for ever and ever. Amen.

ROMANS 5:3–4
We also rejoice in our sufferings, because we know that suffering produces perseverance; perseverance, character; and character, hope.

PATIENCE TO ENDURE HARD TIMES

2 TIMOTHY 2:3
Endure hardship ... like a good soldier of Christ Jesus.

COLOSSIANS 1:10–11
We pray ... that you may live a life worthy of the LORD and may please him in every way: bearing fruit in every good work, growing in the knowledge of God, being strengthened with all power according to his glorious might so that you may have great endurance and patience.

CHAPTER

8

HOW DOES GOD VALUE YOUR RELATIONSHIPS?

Promises for Your Friends and Family

Thank you, God, that you designed me to live in community with others and that you have brought people into my life to challenge, influence, and love me. Thank you that you value my relationships and care about every detail and person in my life. You are a wonderful God.

YOUR FAMILY

EPHESIANS 6:1-3
Children, obey your parents in the LORD, for this is right. "Honor your father and mother"—which is the first commandment with a promise—"that it may go well with you and that you may enjoy long life on the earth."

PSALM 68:5
A father to the fatherless ...
 is God in his holy dwelling.

PSALM 103:13
As a father has compassion on his children,
 so the LORD has compassion on those who fear him.

PSALM 22:10
From birth I was cast upon you;
 from my mother's womb you have been my God.

PSALM 139:13
You created my inmost being, O LORD;
    you knit me together in my mother's womb.

PSALM 127:1
Unless the LORD builds the house,
    its builders labor in vain.

PSALM 103:17
From everlasting to everlasting
    the LORD's love is with those who fear him,
    and his righteousness with their children's children.

PROVERBS 17:6
Children's children are a crown to the aged,
    and parents are the pride of their children.

PROVERBS 6:20–23

Keep your father's commands
and do not forsake your mother's teaching.
Bind them upon your heart forever;
fasten them around your neck.
When you walk, they will guide you;
when you sleep, they will watch over you;
when you awake, they will speak to you.
For these commands are a lamp,
this teaching is a light,
and the corrections of discipline
are the way to life.

ISAIAH 32:18

My people will live in peaceful dwelling places,
in secure homes,
in undisturbed places of rest.

PROVERBS 3:33
The LORD blesses the home of the righteous.

MARK 3:35
Jesus said, "Whoever does God's will is my brother and sister and mother."

PSALM 68:6
God sets the lonely in families.

YOUR MARRIAGE

GENESIS 2:18
The LORD God said, "It is not good for the man to be alone. I will make a helper suitable for him."

MATTHEW 19:4–6
Jesus said, "At the beginning the Creator 'made them male and female,' and said, 'For this reason a man will leave his father and mother and be united to his wife, and the two will become one flesh.' So they are no longer two, but one."

PROVERBS 5:18–19
May your fountain be blessed,
    and may you rejoice in the wife of your youth....
May you ever be captivated by her love.

PROVERBS 18:22
He who finds a wife finds what is good
    and receives favor from the LORD.

PROVERBS 31:10–11, 28–30

A wife of noble character who can find?
    She is worth far more than rubies.
Her husband has full confidence in her
    and lacks nothing of value....
Her children arise and call her blessed;
    her husband also, and he praises her:
"Many women do noble things,
    but you surpass them all."
Charm is deceptive, and beauty is fleeting;
    but a woman who fears the LORD
        is to be praised.

ECCLESIASTES 4:9–10

Two are better than one,
    because they have a good return for their work:
If one falls down,
    his friend can help him up.

SONG OF SONGS 8:7
Many waters cannot quench love;
    rivers cannot wash it away.
If one were to give
    all the wealth of his house for love,
    it would be utterly scorned.

PROVERBS 19:14
Houses and wealth are inherited from parents,
    but a prudent wife is from the LORD.

SONG OF SONGS 7:10
I belong to my lover,
    and his desire is for me.

JAMES 5:16
Confess your sins to each other and pray for each
other so that you may be healed. The prayer of a
righteous man is powerful and effective.

YOUR MARRIAGE

1 CORINTHIANS 13:4-8

Love is patient, love is kind. It does not envy, it does not boast, it is not proud. It is not rude, it is not self-seeking, it is not easily angered, it keeps no record of wrongs. Love does not delight in evil but rejoices with the truth. It always protects, always trusts, always hopes, always perseveres. Love never fails.

PROVERBS 12:4

A wife of noble character is her husband's crown.

YOUR FRIENDS

PROVERBS 18:24

A man of many companions may come to ruin,
> but there is a friend who sticks closer than a brother.

PROVERBS 27:17

As iron sharpens iron,
> so one man sharpens another.

ECCLESIASTES 4:9–10

Two are better than one,
> because they have a good return for their work:

If one falls down,
> his friend can help him up.

GALATIANS 6:2

Carry each other's burdens, and in this way you will fulfill the law of Christ.

PROVERBS 13:20

He who walks with the wise grows wise.

PROVERBS 27:6
Wounds from a friend can be trusted.

MATTHEW 18:20
Jesus said, "For where two or three come together in my name, there am I with them."

JOHN 15:13
"Greater love has no one than this, that he lay down his life for his friends," Jesus told his disciples.

JOHN 15:15
Jesus said, "I no longer call you servants, because a servant does not know his master's business. Instead, I have called you friends, for everything that I learned from my Father I have made known to you."

JOB 16:20–21
My intercessor is my friend
    as my eyes pour out tears to God;
on behalf of a man he pleads with God
    as a man pleads for his friend.

PROVERBS 17:9
He who covers over an offense promotes love,
    but whoever repeats the matter separates
        close friends.

PROVERBS 27:9
Perfume and incense bring joy to the heart,
    and the pleasantness of one's friend
        springs from his earnest counsel.

ECCLESIASTES 4:12
Though one may be overpowered,
    two can defend themselves.
A cord of three strands is not quickly broken.

1 SAMUEL 20:42
Jonathan said to David, "Go in peace, for we have
sworn friendship with each other in the name of the
LORD, saying, 'The LORD is witness between you and
me, and between your descendants and my descendants forever.'"

YOUR FRIENDS

PROVERBS 17:17
A friend loves at all times,
    and a brother is born for adversity.

PROVERBS 22:11
He who loves a pure heart and whose speech is gracious
    will have the king for his friend.

PSALM 34:17–18
The righteous cry out, and the LORD hears them;
    he delivers them from all their troubles.
The LORD is close to the brokenhearted
    and saves those who are crushed in spirit.

YOUR CHURCH

ROMANS 12:4-8

Just as each of us has one body with many members,
and these members do not all have the same function,
so in Christ we who are many form one body, and
each member belongs to all the others. We have different
gifts, according to the grace given us. If a man's gift is
prophesying, let him use it in proportion to his faith. If
it is serving, let him serve; if it is teaching, let him
teach; if it is encouraging, let him encourage; if it is
contributing to the needs of others, let him give
generously; if it is leadership, let him govern diligently;
if it is showing mercy, let him do it cheerfully.

EPHESIANS 4:11-13

It was Christ who gave some to be apostles, some to be
prophets, some to be evangelists, and some to be pastors
and teachers, to prepare God's people for works of
service, so that the body of Christ may be built up until
we all reach unity in the faith and in the knowledge of
the Son of God and become mature, attaining to the
whole measure of the fullness of Christ.

1 CORINTHIANS 12:27
You are the body of Christ, and each one of you is a part of it.

EPHESIANS 2:21–22
In Christ the whole building is joined together and rises to become a holy temple in the LORD. And in him you too are being built together to become a dwelling in which God lives by his Spirit.

1 CORINTHIANS 12:12–13
The body is a unit, though it is made up of many parts; and though all its parts are many, they form one body. So it is with Christ. For we were all baptized by one Spirit into one body—whether Jews or Greeks, slave or free—and we were all given the one Spirit to drink.

JAMES 5:16
Confess your sins to each other and pray for each other so that you may be healed. The prayer of a righteous man is powerful and effective.

EPHESIANS 4:4-6
There is one body and one Spirit—just as you were called to one hope when you were called—one LORD, one faith, one baptism; one God and Father of all, who is over all and through all and in all.

1 CORINTHIANS 12:28-31
In the church God has appointed first of all apostles, second prophets, third teachers, then workers of miracles, also those having gifts of healing, those able to help others, those with gifts of administration, and those speaking in different kinds of tongues. Are all apostles? Are all prophets? Are all teachers? Do all work miracles? Do all have gifts of healing? Do all speak in tongues? Do all interpret? But eagerly desire the greater gifts.

PSALM 133:1
How good and pleasant it is
    when brothers live together in unity!

EPHESIANS 3:10–12
God's intent was that now, through the church, the
manifold wisdom of God should be made known to the
rulers and authorities in the heavenly realms, according
to his eternal purpose which he accomplished in Christ
Jesus our LORD. In him and through faith in him we
may approach God with freedom and confidence.

CHAPTER

9

HOW SHOULD YOU LIVE NOW?

Promises for the Christian Walk

Thank you, my loving Father, that you are not finished with me yet. As you and I journey through this life together, please make me more into your likeness so that you will be satisfied with the person I am becoming in you.

YOUR FINANCES

MALACHI 3:10
"Bring the whole tithe into the storehouse, that there may be food in my house. Test me in this," says the LORD Almighty, "and see if I will not throw open the floodgates of heaven and pour out so much blessing that you will not have room enough for it."

2 CORINTHIANS 9:7
Each man should give what he has decided in his heart to give, not reluctantly or under compulsion, for God loves a cheerful giver.

PROVERBS 3:9–10
Honor the LORD with your wealth,
     with the firstfruits of all your crops;
then your barns will be filled to overflowing,
     and your vats will brim over with new wine.

PHILIPPIANS 4:11–12
I have learned to be content whatever the circumstances. I know what it is to be in need, and I know what it is to have plenty. I have learned the secret of being content in any and every situation, whether well fed or hungry, whether living in plenty or in want.

1 TIMOTHY 6:6
Godliness with contentment is great gain.

PROVERBS 11:28
Whoever trusts in his riches will fall,
    but the righteous will thrive like a green leaf.

MATTHEW 6:31–33
Jesus taught, "Do not worry, saying, 'What shall we eat?' or 'What shall we drink?' or 'What shall we wear?' For the pagans run after all these things, and your heavenly Father knows that you need them. But seek first his kingdom and his righteousness, and all these things will be given to you as well."

PROVERBS 21:20
In the house of the wise are stores of choice food and oil.

PROVERBS 19:1
Better a poor man whose walk is blameless
    than a fool whose lips are perverse.

PHILIPPIANS 4:19
God will meet all your needs according to his glorious riches in Christ Jesus.

LUKE 6:38
Jesus said, "Give, and it will be given to you. A good measure, pressed down, shaken together and running over, will be poured in your lap. For with the measure you use, it will be measured to you."

ROMANS 13:8
Let no debt remain outstanding, except the continuing debt to love one another, for he who loves his fellowman has fulfilled the law.

HEBREWS 13:5
Keep your lives free from the love of money and be content with what you have, because God has said,

> "Never will I leave you;
> never will I forsake you."

PROVERBS 13:11
He who gathers money little by little makes it grow.

ECCLESIASTES 7:12
Wisdom is a shelter
    as a money is a shelter,
but the advantage of knowledge is this:
    that wisdom preserves the life of its possessor.

YOUR WORK

COLOSSIANS 3:23–24
Whatever you do, work at it with all your heart, as working for the LORD, not for men, since you know that you will receive an inheritance from the LORD as a reward.

LUKE 16:10
Whoever can be trusted with very little can also be trusted with much.

1 CORINTHIANS 15:58
Always give yourselves fully to the work of the LORD, because you know that your labor in the LORD is not in vain.

PHILIPPIANS 1:6
God who began a good work in you will carry it on to completion until the day of Christ Jesus.

HEBREWS 4:9–10
There remains ... a Sabbath-rest for the people of God; for anyone who enters God's rest also rests from his own work, just as God did from his.

PROVERBS 10:4
Diligent hands bring wealth.

HEBREWS 13:20–21
May the God of peace, who through the blood of the
eternal covenant brought back from the dead our
LORD Jesus, that great Shepherd of the sheep, equip
you with everything good for doing his will, and may
he work in us what is pleasing to him, through Jesus
Christ, to whom be glory for ever and ever.

PROVERBS 11:3
The integrity of the upright guides them.

HEBREWS 6:10
God is not unjust; he will not forget your work and the
love you have shown him as you have helped his people.

PHILIPPIANS 2:13
It is God who works in you to will and to act according
to his good purpose.

2 CORINTHIANS 9:8

God is able to make all grace abound to you, so that in all things at all times, having all that you need, you will abound in every good work.

1 CORINTHIANS 3:11–14

No one can lay any foundation other than the one already laid, which is Jesus Christ. If any man builds on this foundation using gold, silver, costly stones, wood, hay or straw, his work will be shown for what it is, because the Day will bring it to light. It will be revealed with fire, and the fire will test the quality of each man's work. If what he has built survives, he will receive his reward.

1 CORINTHIANS 3:9

We are God's fellow workers; you are God's field, God's building.

PSALM 41:12

In my integrity you uphold me, O LORD,
    and set me in your presence forever.

YOUR WORK

ECCLESIASTES 5:12
The sleep of a laborer is sweet.

PROVERBS 14:23
All hard work brings a profit.

JOHN 6:27
Jesus said, "Do not work for food that spoils, but for food that endures to eternal life, which the Son of Man will give you. On him God the Father has placed his seal of approval."

CLAY IN THE POTTER'S HANDS

ISAIAH 64:8

O LORD, you are our Father.
>   We are the clay, you are the potter;
>   we are all the work of your hand.

2 CORINTHIANS 4:6–7

God made his light shine in our hearts to give us the light of the knowledge of the glory of God in the face of Christ. But we have this treasure in jars of clay to show that this all-surpassing power is from God and not from us.

PHILIPPIANS 2:12–13

As you have always obeyed—not only in my presence, but now much more in my absence—continue to work out your salvation with fear and trembling, for it is God who works in you to will and to act according to his good purpose.

JEREMIAH 18:6

"Can I not do with you as this potter does?" declares the LORD. "Like clay in the hand of the potter, so are you in my hand."

PHILIPPIANS 1:6
God who began a good work in you will carry it on to completion until the day of Christ Jesus.

PSALM 12:6
The words of the LORD are flawless,
 like silver refined in a furnace of clay,
 purified seven times.

PSALM 138:8
The LORD will fulfill his purpose for me;
 your love, O LORD, endures forever—
 do not abandon the works of your hands.

1 SAMUEL 16:7
The LORD said to Samuel, "The LORD does not look at the things man looks at. Man looks at the outward appearance, but the LORD looks at the heart."

ECCLESIASTES 3:11
God has made everything beautiful in its time.

PSALM 139:13–17
You created my inmost being, O LORD;
    you knit me together in my mother's womb.
I praise you because I am fearfully and wonderfully made;
    your works are wonderful,
    I know that full well.
My frame was not hidden from you
    when I was made in the secret place.
When I was woven together in the depths of the earth,
    your eyes saw my unformed body.
All the days ordained for me
    were written in your book
    before one of them came to be.

How precious to me are your thoughts, O God!
How vast is the sum of them!

GENESIS 1:27–28
God created man in his own image,
    in the image of God he created him;
    male and female he created them.
God blessed them....

CLAY IN THE POTTER'S HANDS

2 TIMOTHY 1:12

I am not ashamed, because I know whom I have believed, and am convinced that God is able to guard what I have entrusted to him for that day.

PSALM 100:3

Know that the LORD is God.

It is he who made us, and we are his;

we are his people, the sheep of his pasture.

RUNNING THE RACE

HEBREWS 12:1
Since we are surrounded by such a great cloud of witnesses, let us throw off everything that hinders and the sin that so easily entangles, and let us run with perseverance the race marked out for us.

ROMANS 5:3–4
We also rejoice in our sufferings, because we know that suffering produces perseverance; perseverance, character; and character, hope.

1 CORINTHIANS 9:27
I beat my body and make it my slave so that after I have preached to others, I myself will not be disqualified for the prize.

REVELATION 2:19
Jesus said, "I know your deeds, your love and faith, your service and perseverance, and that you are now doing more than you did at first."

MATTHEW 24:13
Jesus answered his disciples saying, "He who stands firm to the end will be saved."

MATTHEW 6:19–21
Jesus said to his disciples, "Do not store up for yourselves treasures on earth, where moth and rust destroy, and where thieves break in and steal. But store up for yourselves treasures in heaven, where moth and rust do not destroy, and where thieves do not break in and steal. For where your treasure is, there your heart will be also."

ISAIAH 30:19–21
O people of Zion, who live in Jerusalem, you will weep no more. How gracious the Lord will be when you cry for help! As soon as he hears, he will answer you. Although the Lord gives you the bread of adversity and the water of affliction, your teachers will be hidden no more; with your own eyes you will see them. Whether you turn to the right or to the left, your ears will hear a voice behind you, saying, "This is the way; walk in it."

2 THESSALONIANS 3:5
May the LORD direct your hearts into God's love and Christ's perseverance.

JAMES 1:3–4
The testing of your faith develops perseverance. Perseverance must finish its work so that you may be mature and complete, not lacking anything.

PHILIPPIANS 3:13–14
Forgetting what is behind and straining toward what is ahead, I press on toward the goal to win the prize for which God has called me heavenward in Christ Jesus.

RUNNING THE RACE

EPHESIANS 6:10–13

Be strong in the LORD and in his mighty power. Put on the full armor of God so that you can take your stand against the devil's schemes. For our struggle is not against flesh and blood, but against the rulers, against the authorities, against the powers of this dark world and against the spiritual forces of evil in the heavenly realms. Therefore put on the full armor of God, so that when the day of evil comes, you may be able to stand your ground, and after you have done everything, to stand.

GROWING IN GOD

EPHESIANS 4:15
Speaking the truth in love, we will in all things grow up into him who is the Head, that is, Christ.

MATTHEW 5:13–14
Jesus said to his disciples, "You are the salt of the earth.... You are the light of the world. A city on a hill cannot be hidden."

2 CORINTHIANS 4:6
God, who said, "Let light shine out of darkness," made his light shine in our hearts to give us the light of the knowledge of the glory of God in the face of Christ.

2 CORINTHIANS 4:16–18
We do not lose heart. Though outwardly we are wasting away, yet inwardly we are being renewed day by day. For our light and momentary troubles are achieving for us an eternal glory that far outweighs them all. So we fix our eyes not on what is seen, but on what is unseen. For what is seen is temporary, but what is unseen is eternal.

EPHESIANS 6:14–18

Stand firm then, with the belt of truth buckled around your waist, with the breastplate of righteousness in place, and with your feet fitted with the readiness that comes from the gospel of peace. In addition to all this, take up the shield of faith, with which you can extinguish all the flaming arrows of the evil one. Take the helmet of salvation and the sword of the Spirit, which is the word of God. And pray in the Spirit on all occasions with all kinds of prayers and requests. With this in mind, be alert and always keep on praying for all the saints.

PROVERBS 21:21

He who pursues righteousness and love
    finds life, prosperity and honor.

MATTHEW 5:6

Blessed are those who hunger and thirst for righteous-ness,
    for they will be filled.

GALATIANS 5:22–25

The fruit of the Spirit is love, joy, peace, patience, kindness, goodness, faithfulness, gentleness and self-control. Against such things there is no law. Those who belong to Christ Jesus have crucified the sinful nature with its passions and desires. Since we live by the Spirit, let us keep in step with the Spirit.

JOHN 1:12–13

To all who received Christ, to those who believed in his name, he gave the right to become children of God—children born not of natural descent, nor of human decision or a husband's will, but born of God.

MATTHEW 7:24–25

Jesus said, "Everyone who hears these words of mine and puts them into practice is like a wise man who built his house on the rock. The rain came down, the streams rose, and the winds blew and beat against that house; yet it did not fall, because it had its foundation on the rock."

1 JOHN 4:4
The one who is in you is greater than the one who is in the world.

2 PETER 3:18
Grow in the grace and knowledge of our LORD and Savior Jesus Christ. To him be glory both now and forever.

JOHN 15:5
Jesus said, "I am the vine; you are the branches. If a man remains in me and I in him, he will bear much fruit; apart from me you can do nothing."

HEAVEN: YOUR ULTIMATE REWARD

MATTHEW 5:11–12

Jesus said, "Blessed are you when people insult you, persecute you and falsely say all kinds of evil against you because of me. Rejoice and be glad, because great is your reward in heaven."

MATTHEW 6:20–21

Jesus said to his disciples, "Store up for yourselves treasures in heaven, where moth and rust do not destroy, and where thieves do not break in and steal. For where your treasure is, there your heart will be also."

MATTHEW 10:32

Jesus said, "Whoever acknowledges me before men, I will also acknowledge him before my Father in heaven."

PHILIPPIANS 3:20–21

Our citizenship is in heaven. And we eagerly await a Savior from there, the LORD Jesus Christ, who, by the power that enables him to bring everything under his control, will transform our lowly bodies so that they will be like his glorious body.

2 PETER 3:13

In keeping with God's promise we are looking forward to a new heaven and a new earth, the home of righteousness.

2 PETER 3:13
In keeping with God's promise we are looking forward to a new heaven and a new earth, the home of righteousness.

1 THESSALONIANS 4:16–17
The LORD himself will come down from heaven, with a loud command, with the voice of the archangel and with the trumpet call of God, and the dead in Christ will rise first. After that, we who are still alive and are left will be caught up together with them in the clouds to meet the LORD in the air. And so we will be with the LORD forever.

REVELATION 21:1–5
I saw a new heaven and a new earth, for the first heaven and the first earth had passed away, and there was no longer any sea. I saw the Holy City, the new Jerusalem, coming down out of heaven from God, prepared as a bride beautifully dressed for her husband. And I heard a loud voice from the throne saying, "Now the dwelling of God is with men, and he will live with them. They will be his people, and God himself will be with them and be their God. He will wipe every tear from their eyes. There will be no more death or mourning or crying or pain, for the old order of things has passed away."
He who was seated on the throne said, "I am making everything new!"

1 PETER 1:3–5

Praise be to the God and Father of our LORD Jesus Christ! In his great mercy he has given us new birth into a living hope through the resurrection of Jesus Christ from the dead, and into an inheritance that can never perish, spoil or fade—kept in heaven for you, who through faith are shielded by God's power until the coming of the salvation that is ready to be revealed in the last time.

ISAIAH 65:17–19

This is what the LORD says,
"Behold, I will create
    new heavens and a new earth.
The former things will not be remembered,
    nor will they come to mind.
But be glad and rejoice forever
    in what I will create,
for I will create Jerusalem to be a delight
    and its people a joy."

HEAVEN: YOUR ULTIMATE REWARD

The Bible is God's chart for you to steer by, to

keep you from the bottom of the sea, and to

show you where the harbor is, and how to

reach it without running on rocks and bars.

Henry Ward Beecher

*My heart is full, L*ORD *God,*

full of your love,

full of your wisdom,

full of your faithfulness,

full of your peace,

all because of your wonderful promises.

Thank you for the privilege to call upon

them to meet all my needs and keep me

always drawing closer to you.

At Inspirio we love to hear from you—
your stories, your feedback,
and your product ideas.
Please send your comments to us
by way of email at
icares@zondervan.com
or to the address below:

i n s p i r i o

Attn: Inspirio Cares
5300 Patterson Avenue SE
Grand Rapids, MI 49530

If you would like further information
about Inspirio and the products we
create please visit us at:
www.inspiriogifts.com

Thank you and God bless!